The Frog
Who Never
Became
a Prince

The Frog Who Never Became a Prince

An Adult Book for "Performing" Christians

James "Frog" Sullivan

VISION HOUSE PUBLISHERS
Santa Ana, California 92705

Contents

Foreword

James "Frog" Sullivan is a real person. Literally hundreds of high school boys and girls, many of them now men and women, will never be the same because they ran into a man with a gravelly voice and a quick smile at a baseball game, in the halls at school, or on the football field at a weekend camp. Somehow Frog always managed to cross those tough invisible age lines between high schoolers and their elders without losing either rapport or respect. And both the kids and their parents knew that something unusual had happened in his life. He doesn't just "like young people." He believes that life can be different for them — better and more creatively whole — than it has been for many of their parents.

This book tells two stories. One is an exciting race against time and one of the most devastating hurricanes ever to hit the Texas Gulf Coast. Frog is trying to get home to his wife, Carolyn, through the storm at night. The other story is his life relived during that wild ride toward home.

Having known the author for years I am pleased to be able to take part in launching his first book. I have heard him tell his story and watched him live it. He has helped me personally and stood by me as a friend. This book is a witness to what God can do in changing a tough kid's direction and motivating a gifted man to spend over twenty years giving his life to help young people to find God and wholeness.

Keith Miller
Port Aransas, Texas

Receipt

...obile and Outreach Services
...-278-5100 x.204
www.mc-npl.org

Wednesday, September 2, 2015 1:28:02 PM

Title: THE FROG WHO NEVER BECAME A PRINCE
Due: 09/16/2015

Title: Does this beach make me look fat? [sound recording]
Due: 09/30/2015

Title: The job [sound recording]
Due: 09/30/2015

Total items: 3

Thank you for your MC-NPL Bookmobile
and Outreach Services Patronage!

Preface

There's a great deal of talk in some Christian circles today about kissing frogs and turning frogs into princes. I don't believe this is the mission of the church. As I see it, the true greatness of God's love helps frogs be frogs.

I don't consider myself a frog, I consider myself a person; but my nickname "Frog" has had a lot to do with who I am. I earned it while in junior high school because of the way I ran. For years I not only tried to change the name, I tried to change the person. Somewhere down the line I got the idea that once you become a Christian all your ugliness and all your problems go away, and you become perfect. It was like a kiss that the princess bestows upon the frog transforming him into someone beautiful. As a result, I could accept neither the "frogness" nor the "princeness" in my life.

I conceived the idea that because the Bible says "you will be changed," I would become somebody else. All my problems would go away, and all my relationships would become perfect. Of course, this sort of thinking never allowed for anything but the perfect marriage: my wife and I would live in a beautiful castle surrounded by the moat of God's love, and the world would never get across to harm us.

I learned instead that when the Christian commits himself to God, he is open to a life of involvement. People can walk in and out freely; he gets hurt; his family gets hurt; his children are hurt; his wife gets hurt; they both get torn apart by misunderstandings. The Christian faith does not guarantee immunity from troubles; it does guarantee that no matter what happens God is deeply involved in my life, and I must trust him with it.

As you read this book, remember it is merely the struggles of a frog to become something he was never supposed to be. Every person I ever met that was truly outstanding, I wanted to be like. And, all along, God was saying, "Hey! Frog Sullivan, I love *you*. You don't have to be somebody else." It took me a long time to learn that lesson, and I hope that what has happened to me, to Carolyn, and to our relationships might be of some help to you.

It would be impossible to list the name of every person who encouraged this project, but I gratefully acknowledge these friends and colleagues who helped put it all together:

Steve Stone and Frankie Blalock Hardy, who heard the first tapes and urged me to continue writing,

Carolyn Kellum, who transcribed the tapes and typed the first draft,

Bita Moss, who corrected my grammar and helped give form and substance to the story,

Shirley Welch, my secretary, who spent hours making corrections,

Keith Miller, who said from the beginning, "You have to share your life in writing with other people,"

Young Life and the staff, who continue to enrich my life after many years, and to the present staff with whom I interact daily,

Bill Cody, Leonard Holloway, Sam Fore, and the HEB family,

Howard and Barbara Dean, warm friends,

And thousands of kids whose vitality and spiritual energy has been a constant source of inspiration.

"FROG" SULLIVAN

1
Getting Ready

That day, August 3, 1970, was a happy one for me. My daughter, Cathy, was enjoying herself in California visiting some friends. Scott, my son, was a camper here, where he wanted to be more than any other place in the world. And my wife, Carolyn, was home in Portland, Texas, getting ready to start teaching in about two weeks. All was at peace in my world. I was feeling some deep sense of security . . . one of those times in my life when I felt that everything was okay. I was looking forward to the day and being involved with the staff and the kids God had given us to work with.

If I had known early on that beautiful, typical, hill-country day that home was going to be a reality for me for the first time, I probably would not have panicked as much as I did as the day wore on. It started like most summer days in South Texas on the Edwards Plateau — with its old oaks and mesquites, some of the finest pasture land in that part of the world, and its beautiful cool rivers that cut through the plateau to make it some of the prettiest country in the world.

Situated down inside one of those pretty, gouged-out areas is a beautiful camp called Echo Valley, part of the HEB Foundation camps at Leakey, Texas. That particular morning began like a typical first day of a camp session with bright, energetic kids from all over the southwestern United States, happy, frantic, and loud, looking for fun and excitement and things to do. The sun was warm, the sky was blue, one of those days that was so perfect it made you wonder what was going to happen. I awakened the kids, screaming and yelling at them like I always do at camp in the morning: "All right, out of the rack, you crazy kids. Let's go! You know we've got some living to do . . .

we've got some fun to have and breakfast in forty-five minutes. Let's go!"

As I walked down to the kitchen to eat breakfast and drink a cup of coffee with my staff, reflections ran through my mind of how I had gotten involved working with the kids in this camp. A few years ago Bill Cody had talked to me about helping with the program, including camping. We had grown from thirteen campers at our first session six years ago to about one hundred campers in this session. I remembered all the great kids I've known and loved and have been able to share God's love with.

I guess the most memorable thing about the camps is what has happened to my life and to the life of a friend of mine named Keith Miller, who had invited me to participate in a week's program at Laity Lodge, which is just up the river about a mile. Keith and I had been friends for a long time in Oklahoma City, but now I was living far away, near Corpus Christi, Texas. Nevertheless, we had stayed close to each other! In some ways my life had been tremendously changed in that Laity Lodge camp setting and through my work with the kids there.

Throughout that day, all of us at camp, including the kids primarily from Corpus Christi, became increasingly concerned about reports of the hurricane that was in the Gulf of Mexico. Early newscasts indicated that it was not a bad hurricane, but that it was going to come into Corpus Christi, that the eye would pass directly over Corpus. Some of the kids began to call home to check with their parents. Their families reassured them: It was not going to be bad . . . they were okay . . . just go ahead and have fun. And if they needed them, they would get in touch.

Carolyn was in the middle of making plans for her prospective work week at school when I called to ask if she was okay. She said yes and that the neighbors' boys were helping her tape up the windows and that she was all right. I encouraged her to leave and drive on up to the hill country. She said no, that she didn't think the hurricane was going to be that bad. They had named it Celia; it had been out in the gulf for a long time and it was small. Although it was well organized and compact, they didn't think it was going to be a really bad one. The winds were then somewhere around seventy-five miles an hour; they expected that as it moved in closer to the coast, it would probably decrease in intensity. So I told her I would call her later on and went on back to the business of being with the kids . . . enjoying them . . . having fun.

Carolyn and I had been married for seventeen years. After I hung up the phone, I realized why she wouldn't leave Corpus: Our house there was the first *real* home we had ever owned. It was a beautiful home that we had built in Portland. Neither one of us had grown up with much as far as material things were concerned. And *that* home was Carolyn's castle, something she had helped put together, plan, and she loved it very much. Material possessions meant a lot to us at this time, probably because we had never had them before.

As I thought about that, I got even more concerned. Carolyn would try to stay in that house and hold it together no matter what happened. I guess during the morning and early afternoon I called her three or four times and talked to her about it. She said she was okay, she was going to stick it out. I even called Ted Anderson and some other friends of ours in Corpus, and the weather bureau. I listened to the car radio for reports, well aware that Carolyn would not leave because she felt that as long as she could stay there, everything would be all right and nothing would happen to the house. We had never been through a hurricane. The weather bureau kept saying that they didn't think the storm was going to be quite that bad. Most people in Corpus ride those things out; they board up their houses, put tape on their windows, and wait for the wind and the rain. Nobody was aware, I guess, of the impending disaster.

Being the kind of person I am and have been most of my life, very ego oriented and carrying around a lot of guilt, especially in my relationship with Carolyn — I became extremely anxious. Around one o'clock we stopped getting any of the radio stations from Corpus; so we switched to San Antonio stations. We learned that the hurricane had approached Corpus and evidently was pretty bad; all communication with Portland was lost. The weather bureau in San Antonio was saying that the eye of the hurricane had passed over the coastline and was approaching Port Aransas, Aransas Pass, Ingleside, Portland, and then would head up to Odem, Mathis, and out into the South Texas cattle country . . . and then into Mexico.

My concern grew with every new detail; finally we heard that Celia had hit the coast around 2:50 P.M. All power was knocked out; communication was impossible. The authorities continued trying to make contact, but they couldn't enter the hurricane to do so. They'd just have to wait until someone could get in and find out what was going on to get the news out. My anxiety level skyrocketed, and my guilt feelings were having a heyday. But I faked it with the kids, telling them I thought everything was okay, that just the power lines were down . . . that we should begin to find out something later on in the afternoon . . . we'd check. So we went on about our activities.

It was still blue skies and sunshine in the hill country, and the kids were having fun. During dinner we listened to the radio, trying desperately to find out what was happening. Not much information! About 7:30 or 8:00 that night we began to get some reports from radio stations in San Antonio. They were trying to describe the situation in Corpus Christi and in the surrounding communities. None were official reports, however. Radio and police vans, army reserves, and a medical station had developed some kind of communication and were beginning to get word to the outside. The first reports were really bad!

There was no way to get in or out of Corpus, either. We kept trying to make phone calls. The kids were upset, really worried about their parents and homes. They were beginning to cry, and we could find out very little about what was happening. I believe that the first communication really came from ham operators who had put their sets back together, gotten some emergency power, and had begun to talk with the radio stations in San Antonio. They were beginning to report some of the damage they had seen. One of the reports that we heard almost immediately was that downtown Corpus Christi was virtually destroyed — and I lived only *eleven miles* from downtown Corpus! I guess I figured that Portland had probably blown away; and Carolyn and the house — well, I didn't have any idea what might have happened to them. The kids were distraught; what about their families — and their friends? I was wrestling with the idea of trying to get home to find out what had happened. In my compulsiveness I decided to do just that.

I began getting things organized to leave. Finally about 11:00 P.M. when the radio came on, the announcers said that they had been able to get word from Aransas Pass, Port Aransas, Gregory, Ingleside, and Portland. These communities were almost 100 percent damaged, homes and roofs gone; people had been taken to the hospitals, injured. These were not official reports, but, man, I didn't know that! I was going out of my mind!!! At that point I jumped in my car — which was really Carolyn's car, a beautiful Buick, a good car, plenty fast — and I told the kids that as soon as I could, I'd let them know what was going on.

I pulled out the front gate on 83 and headed south at 11:30 P.M. It's a four-and-a-half-hour drive from Leakey, Texas, to Portland, Texas. I shoved the accelerator to the floorboard and immediately was at 120 miles per hour. I was in a state of panic — to think that I had let this terrible thing happen to Carolyn. Once again I was not with her in a major emergency of our lives . . . and now I had let her get killed.

Beginnings 2

Most of my life, I guess, I have felt just outside the front gate. Maybe out the front gate symbolizes beginnings, which are really hard for me. I have struggled with my insides — who I am, what I want to be, and where I've wanted to go. The last fifteen or twenty years have been significant, but before that I never really considered myself anything. So many people have touched me; so many people have meant so much to me. Out of beginnings grow significant relationships that help us understand other

Christians who are struggling to live and to give. And their struggles encourage us to commit our lives to Christ in a world that is confused, lonely, hurting on the inside. I guess I understood about the emotional pain from the time that I was a little kid because I was confused and lonely, and I remember hurting a lot.

As I pulled out the gate and headed for home, I began thinking of some of the great things in my life — one of the greatest being that in some magical way I'd learned that redemption doesn't save us from ourselves. Redemption in Christ's love saves us and helps us to know ourselves and to live with ourselves. It was in this state that I rushed toward the little community of Leakey. Some of what I was as a kid flashed across my mind . . .

Born in a relatively poor family with little education, my father a laborer for the Ford Motor Company, I grew up in a tough neighborhood. And I had a hard time growing up! My mother and father, I believe, loved me. I don't remember just how they communicated this, but somehow I know I was loved. I was the second of four boys, the eldest of whom they loved more than they did the rest of us. I don't recall much about my childhood, especially through the first six years of school. My school life was so miserable that I probably blotted it out intentionally. I flunked the first, third, and seventh grades — not being good at much of anything in school except getting into trouble.

My dad drank heavily on the weekends. As a little child, I heard my mother and dad arguing loudly and mother crying. At that age I was an unhappy, insecure person, and I wanted to run away. Outwardly I began to develop a carefree attitude, but there was a lot I cared about. I cared very much about my dad. I still remember picking him up off the front porch one night, dragging him into the living room, and laying him on the couch. But he was a hard worker, and there was always food on the table even though we didn't have a bathtub indoors, or plumbing in our house, until I was in high school. I developed a low frustration point, coupled with confusion and loneliness, and by the time I was approaching fourteen, I began to have serious headaches from this condition. A lot of nights my head hurt so bad that I'd cry myself to sleep. Some nights my mom would rub my back, my neck, and put cold towels on my forehead to try to ease the pain. This is about the only concrete experience of direct love that I can recall from my childhood.

I wasn't encouraged much about school, and as I already said, I flunked the first, third, and seventh grades. I didn't like it, didn't want any part of it. I wanted to run away from school and from all the confusion that existed in my family. When I was only twelve years old, one Saturday morning my father poured me my first drink at the breakfast table and told me that he wanted me to learn to drink from him and not from my friends. I felt terribly frustrated and very confused about becoming what he was. I remember wanting to get out of there, and yet knowing that I was trapped. I did so want to become a man!

I don't recall many names of the kids I knew then, but they, too, seemed unhappy. In junior high school my outlook on life changed for the better when I had my first male teacher — a man with whom I quickly identified. I felt he was the first real man I'd met. He was a P.E. teacher and a coach, and he offered me something I'd never before had in my life — an opportunity to participate in sports. He talked me into playing football and baseball and running track. I think those things became anxiety-reducers for me. I wanted so to hit people, and now I learned to hit people with pads on — to run over people and to knock them down. It was my way of saying to the world, "You've done me dirt; so I'm going to beat the hell out of you this way."

About this same time I joined a crowd called the "Binghampton Buzzards." Our primary goal was to roll drunks and beat up Negroes, taking their paychecks. Anything else we wanted done, we did. We beat up people and rolled homosexuals for what they were worth, as a matter of course. We would do anything for a few bucks, and I was pretty much a part of all this. This crowd began to introduce a lot of things to a lot of other kids as well. Alcohol was an important part of our lives. It was easy to get; all we had to do was pay some poor old Negro fellow twenty-five cents and he would buy us a fifth of cheap wine or some kind of booze or beer — or we would steal it ourselves. We also stole other things and sold them to make the money to buy booze. At fifteen years of age I was practically an alcoholic. There was not a weekend in my life from eighth grade until my senior year of high school that I wasn't drunk. Also, at this same time, I was introduced to girls for whom I learned to have little respect. They were just things to be used for satisfaction.

It's hard to put into words what a confused,

mixed-up kid I was. I think the bitterness of my life was beginning to eat me alive. I knew what I was and I didn't want to be that — yet there was no escape. There was no way to get away! There was no place to run! No one to run to! I couldn't think of anyone in my whole life who loved me or cared about me.

Church! It was never discussed or even mentioned except maybe on Easter Sunday, Mother's Day, or something like that. It was at this time that my big brother, whom I admired as a beautiful athlete, was shot up in the Pacific in World War II. He came home a broken, hurt person. I was going into my sophomore year of high school when he returned. The two of us got drunk almost every night. I watched us as if from afar as we destroyed ourselves . . . all the time not being able to do anything about it.

In the middle of the fall of my sophomore year, I quit high school. This meant giving up football, the one thing I loved the most, but I thought if I could make enough money I could move out of that house. Then I would change and everything would be different. But I went from bad to worse. Part of that year I lived with a woman who was about twenty-five years old, and I was just a kid seventeen. But eventually some of the right things began to happen. For one thing, I reached the bottom of the pit. I realized with stark clarity that I was nothing! And was most likely going to continue to be nothing! Sometimes I wanted to kill myself, and that scared me. But deep down I knew that I did *not* want to destroy my life — I just did not want to be a nobody. I wanted to be somebody.

Desperation overcame me, and I became consciously aware of the need for someone to love me, someone to care. I had never been able to find this deep caring with girls, or among any of my friends. They were so hung-up on fighting, beating up people, getting drunk, and destroying . . . and so was I. But my stomach was turning sour from the futility of it all.

*   *   *

Almost immediately the street lights, what two or three lights are on in Leakey in the summertime, blasted across my car as I hit a high rate of speed. My mind was racing about as fast as my car, but the lights brought me back to reality, and I became aware of heading home to try to find my wife to see if she was okay. Unnoticed, I sped through Leaky with its rolled-up-at-seven sidewalks. Pedal back down

to the floorboard, I headed home to Portland as
fast as that car would go, my mind going back
and forth from reality to where I'd come from.
Maybe this was the trip, the ultimate . . . the
journey that would bring me closer to my loved
ones and closer to my own family. I remember
that as I left Leaky I began to think back to how
I'd gotten there . . .

3
Frog
Becomes
a Real Frog

What had touched my life to make me the hopped-up, anxious, mixed-up person that I'd been most of my days? I guess a lot of it happened in my high-school years. Even though I had dropped out of school, I still wanted to go back, still wanted to play football, which I loved. At this point a person came into my life who seemed to love. A teacher talked to me about going back to school. She tutored me so that I could pass the courses and enter the eleventh grade instead of the tenth. I think that it was then that God began to get through to me. I didn't know it was God yet, but I needed something, and I began to experience love and concern through this wonderful lady's life. She loved me and showed that she believed in me as a person, something no one else had been able to do. There is no way I can say what her caring about me meant.

I went back to high school to prove that I was a man. Can you believe that I ran track and played football and didn't weigh 135 pounds soaking wet? This driving urge to be a man really ripped up my entire personality, marked my life so that scars on my body and the doubting feelings I had about myself caused me many unhappy hours and times of frustration. But I desperately needed to show the gang, myself, and everybody else that I could be my own man.

In my junior year I began to have fun! Although I came close to some people in athletics, my drinking continued, our beating up on people continued. My attitude about taking things out on others and looking for kicks at their expense continued. But for some reason, some of us began to get close to one another. Even now I know where one or two of those fellows are. I learned to love those guys, and I think they began to love me a little. We had some hilarious times together. Nights when we'd be smashed out of our minds, so smashed that we didn't know where we were or what we were doing, we'd end up in West Memphis. I pushed a friend of mine through a plate-glass window to save him from a cop. We worked at having the wildest, craziest adventures that were humanly possible.

*   *   *

At this time, 1946, another great thing happened — into my life walked a fantastic idea called "Young Life." Although some of my friends started the group at our high school, they could never get me to go. I can recall meeting the guys at the old Cotton Boll Tavern in Memphis after Young Life dismissed, and saying, "Well, what did you guys do tonight?"

And they would answer, "We went to Young Life!"

Then I'd want to know what they did there, and they'd say, "Had some fun, sang some songs, and the leader talked to us."

"What did he talk about?" I'd want to know.

"Well," they'd answer, "talked to us about the Bible."

And I'd just crack up laughing: "He knows you guys are the biggest bunch of phonies I've ever been around in my life. You're drunk every weekend, and now you're going to church on Tuesday nights."

I wondered why all those guys were going and what was happening. Then one of my best friends and I had a knock-down, drag-out fight. We had it one afternoon, and I knew he went to Young Life every Tuesday night. So I got a date with his girlfriend and headed for my first Young Life meeting, knowing that when I walked in the door it would cause the biggest commotion they probably ever had at a Young Life club.

I waited until everybody had arrived and club had started. When it was going full-blast, I knocked. Somebody opened the door; there were about 125 kids sitting around on the floor. The director was leading a discussion, and everyone was talking. Some of my best friends got up and let the girl in, and then everyone started talking at once. I didn't know what Young Life was at this stage or what in the world was going on. The leader knew me, and he knew my reputation. After restoring order, he asked me to come right in and sit down. I waited and watched this wild thing. Kids were singing Christian songs like crazy, as if they really meant the words. They read out of the Bible and chatted something about life from its pages. My response to the whole thing was: What in the world is going on here? We hadn't gone to church much, and I didn't know anything about Christ or God. They were both just cuss words to me. As far as being a Christian or being around Christians, I couldn't imagine what I would do. We were known as the bad Sullivans in our neighborhood, and most people stayed away from us, especially on Sundays. There was a church on every block, but I never attended or knew much about the people who did. I don't recall ever seeing a minister from one of those churches in our home.

I went back the next week to participate in this little Young Life club, not knowing why . . . maybe because the leader seemed to show a personal interest in me. And I was told later by one of the Young Life staff that the club leaders got together that night after club, in their car, and prayed that one of two things would happen to me. First, that I would continue to come and that I would become a true Christian and give my life to Jesus Christ. Or that I would quit coming, for if there was one person that could destroy the solidity of the club for Tech

High, I was that person! That's the kind of reputation I had built.

In the spring of my junior year I went to Young Life — yet I don't remember much of what was said or any of the songs that were sung or what was going on. I realized that Howard Kee, our club leader, loved me and was interested in who I was and what I was doing. I didn't know *why* he did, but he began to get to me. One night I was almost embarrassed when he called me aside after club and said they were going to have a weekend camp, and he would like for me to go and do a little lifeguarding. The didn't need me to lifeguard; this was a con game. He was just sharing with me so that he could get the money for me to go, because he knew I didn't have it. I asked if some of my buddies could come along. He said, "Well, get them and go!"

So a cabin full of guys went to Chickasaw State Park where Young Life camped on weekends. There were eight or nine of us in our cabin — a couple were high-school all-American football players and one was a national Golden Gloves finalist in Chicago. All of those great big studs . . . *and me*. We had brought our cards and our booze, preparing to do our thing. As we got out our bottles that first night and prepared to start our card game, we heard singing in the background. The meeting had started in the main building.

Presently a stocky, well-built man appeared in the doorway. "Put up the cards, put up the booze — we're going to have a meeting!" I said to myself, "Buddy, you're dead!" And I kept waiting for one of our guys to kill him. But there was something about him that was very different from any other man I had met before. We could tell that this man wasn't fooling; he meant what he said. We just put up everything, and one by one, all of us sheepishly walked over to the meeting. There was something in this man that was for real. He was George Sheffer, one of the five guys that joined Jim Rayburn to get Young Life going all over the country. Maybe I sensed it . . . that he really liked us and cared about us and he certainly wanted us where the rest of the kids were that night. I went to that meeting, sat on the floor with everybody else. I don't remember who talked, but I sat there listening to the singing with about a hundred or more kids.

That night I heard one of the greatest messages I'd ever heard. What I didn't know and nobody had found it necessary to tell me was that Jesus Christ loved me — so much so that he came down here and lived and died and arose again to give his life for me, one of the dirtiest kids that had ever been around his earth. That night has to be one of the most significant events in my life. I did some powerful thinking, for I felt that something needed to happen in my life after that. I wasn't sure, though, what they were talking about, and I wasn't sure what it was going to cost if I took it seriously. And yet I listened to this unbelievable message: "God loves me!" I was desperate, screaming with everything in my being for life and for realness and wholesomeness. Maybe that's why I was thinking that God was the answer. He needed to come into my life. Maybe I saw him only as an escape from the affair of who I was and the loneliness of the kind of life I was living — the fear that I was going to become something that I didn't want to become.

I saw the Christian faith as an opportunity to get outside myself and become something worthwhile. That Saturday night at that little old camp, I went outside the cabin, and for the first time in my life, I prayed. I talked to God saying something like this: "God, I don't know very much about you. But if you're up there and you do indeed love me like they tell me you do, then you'll come into my life and do something for me and somehow I'll try to do something for you in return. I don't know what it will be. I don't know much about you, or what you want, but I'm going to try. I'm going to give my life for you."

I opened my heart and gave my life to Christ that night. No fireworks went off, but I think, as a friend of mine summed it up later, I felt clean on the inside for the first time. Yes, for the first time in my whole life I really was clean! It was a *good* clean, and something that Frog Sullivan needed desperately in his life. I'm not sure what happened that night, but it was a beginning of something and beginnings are hard. There was some newness though, and I guess maybe, for the time being, I thought some good thoughts about myself. If God could love me, then I must be important; I must be somebody. Maybe for the first time that night I went to sleep confident and secure, not knowing, like most kids, that a simple commitment could mean some drastic changes later.

4
The New Image: Jim Rayburn

Still struggling with my initial commitment to Christ, I went home from Young Life camp to face the crowd. I was nineteen years old and in the spring semester of my junior year in high school. As I grappled with important decisions and began to try to discover who I was and why I existed, I went from bad to worse.

My oldest brother, who was once again trying to play professional baseball, became involved in my life. We spent a wild spring and summer, working and drinking. I had very little to do with Christ then although I believe my initial encounter was the spark that was later to catch on. That summer, Young Life had a camp, and I was invited to go. It was the last week of summer vacation before fall football practice began, and I knew I needed to get in shape. But I remembered that brief experience with God. I was still liking it and wanted to taste more. I wanted to find out if he was for real.

I went to camp, and there met the man who was to become the greatest single influence of my life, Jim Rayburn, the founder and head of Young Life. He was the counselor in my cabin, and he talked with us every night. He shared his life, he gave us himself, and he influenced me in a way that no other human being had ever done. In that week I found that indeed God was for real, Jesus Christ was for real, and I gave him as much of my life as I knew how.

And that's when things began to happen. I mean, the experience got me to doing something that I didn't want to do. At the end of that week, Jim Rayburn asked me to go with him to Colorado. That meant not playing football in my senior year because I would miss the days of preseason practice. But when I weighed this against the possibilities of personal growth that I thought a week with Jim Rayburn might bring, the decision was obvious: I quit. I gave up football and stayed in Colorado for a week at Star Ranch outside Colorado Springs. I spent that week studying the Bible, and I watched the Young Life staff. There were kids from all over the southwestern part of the United States. By the middle of the week I realized I had to live the rest of my life for God. Somehow I had to be his person and do his will. I didn't know what price God was going to ask me to pay, but I decided then that I was willing to give my life to him and start living his life in my experience from that day forward.

I was growing, studying, learning things about myself. I was also aware that for the first time in my life I was beginning to experience some real happiness and understanding about the kind of person I was and wanted to mature into. Driving back to Memphis, I talked to Howard Kee and the others about how I wanted to make an impact on my high school; how I wanted my friends to find Jesus Christ the way I'd found him — as the one who could meet the needs of their lives, and the one who could go deep where they needed him to do something for them. We prayed and prayed, saying: "Somehow, God, I'll be your person this year." Of course, I didn't know what I was saying, and

I didn't know what I was asking, for God took me up on it.

The next day when I walked into the halls of my high school, those kids knew that I had become a Christian; they all knew that something had happened to me. They could see it in my eyes, in my walk, and in the person that I was. I remember an English teacher looking at me and saying: "I don't know what has happened to you Frog Sullivan, but you're not the same person I used to know." She continued, "I like what I see!" Of course the crowd I ran around with began to kid me and give me a hard time. "Hey, Christian, come on, preach us a message!" I'd never said one word to any of those guys about the fact that I had become a Christian. I never even made any attempt to verbally witness to them nor did I care to. They had already seen the change in a matter of days. The next few months were a real struggle. I loved those guys and wanted to be a part of them; yet they were testing me constantly, trying me like I'd never been tried in my life. Open bets were being taken in the halls of Tech High School as to how long I would last as a Christian.

It was the big joke of that school; guys left bottles in my locker. But deep down inside, I knew that I had found my place, what I wanted and what I wanted to be, and I was willing to pay the price to keep it. In those days, God came to me in a very special way. He put his hand on me and protected me. For the first time since I was in the tenth grade, I went about six months without taking a drink. I was elected president of the Young Life club at Tech High School, a club with previous attendance of fifty kids a week. Immediately that club went to two hundred, or possibly even two hundred fifty kids each week. Things began to happen in my school. Since it was considered the worst high school in Memphis — a tough bunch of kids — it was amazing that within a short period of about three months, many were referring to it as a Christian high school. A lot of my friends began to warm up to Jesus Christ and Young Life leadership, which made me happy. And a lot of those same friends began to open their hearts and their lives to Jesus Christ.

For hours I talked with our leaders about the struggles and the problems going on in my life. For one thing, I didn't know how to treat a girl. Every thought I had about them was bad. I'd never had a real date until my senior year in high school. From the first of September that year until the junior-senior prom the following

spring, I stayed away from girls because I knew
that I couldn't keep my hands off them. But this
was to be a great year for me since, for the first
time, I studied. But it was almost too late. It was
the first time I had really enjoyed *living* life.
One night I stayed home and talked to my
mother and daddy — something I hadn't done
in years — while my mother kept asking if I felt
well, why I didn't go some place.

It was about then, I believe, that I came to
care for people. The Young Life staff had spent
a lot of time with me, sharing their lives with
me. They encouraged me to study the Bible,
which I knew nothing about. I had finally
grown slightly in the Christian faith. I was
beginning to learn to love my mother and
daddy and to love the kids with whom I was
running around. In fact, it became a joke with
the old crowd that they could all get smashed
good because "Ole Frog will take us home." I
never left my friends, for they were still as they
had been: very much a part of my life. As a
result of being involved with these fellows and
caring for them, I saw a lot of them open their
lives to God. A lot of good things began to
happen to me; I was having a great year, and I
even began to think of going to college. But at
the end of my senior year I became frustrated

because I knew I could not make it in college. Yet I knew that if I wanted to have an effective witness for Christ in any area of responsibility, I would have to go to college.

I had no study habits; I was a slow, ineffective reader, and I couldn't write very well. I was the product of a system that kept passing people from one grade to the next just to get rid of them. But I had committed myself to God, and I believed that he had committed himself to me. Fortunately Jim Rayburn invited me to come to Colorado Springs, Colorado, and live in his home with him and his family. I could go to Colorado Springs High School, take some courses; I knew that was what I needed to do. Jim Rayburn was surely a great man, and he was to become the father-figure to me. As I lived in their home and ate at their table, I began to learn so much more about relationships and about love. We lived on a small ranch about six miles from Colorado Springs, with no transportation. I worked every day, read and studied at night. I took a couple of courses at the local high school, postgraduate type courses, and these were good times for me — times of being alone and beginning to find out who I was.

There were plenty of things for me to do,

and work took on a whole new meaning. My mother and father couldn't understand my feelings about leaving home to go to Colorado. They thought I ought to get a job, go to work like all my friends, and eventually get married and just do that with my life . . . no more. That, and just that, was not what I wanted for my life! Somehow I didn't believe that was what God wanted for me either. I began to find out about the Bible and what it had to say. I read, studied, memorized verses, and began to read other books with the Bible. I began to find out how other people thought.

I spent a lot of time with Jim Rayburn. We talked together at length; we read, and we prayed. Many times he shared the burden of the growing pains of Young Life, a vibrant movement trying to explode into existence. Its terrific burden of leadership, and its financial and organizational problems were upon Jim's shoulders. But he had a burning vision that every high-school fellow and girl in America had the right to know the truth about Jesus Christ and his love. He felt that he had to do everything he could to get that message to as many kids as possible. Sometimes we would just get together and laugh. But many times I saw this man on his knees, giving himself to God for the mission of Young Life.

I watched and loved this man for twenty years. At times, it was hard for me, however. Because we were so close, Jim would never let me grow up as a leader. To Jim Rayburn, and to a lot of the Young Life staff, even today, I remain that crummy little kid who graduated from Tech High School, that crummy little kid who grew up on the wrong side of town. Meanwhile, though, I watched Jim Rayburn sacrifice everything to develop the mission of Young Life, the mission that believes that teenagers have the right to know from an adult about the love of God. That you can't expect kids to come to where the message is, you have to take the message to where they are. You have to get to know them and to love them, to become their friend. Then in the context of that friendship and that relationship, you begin to share the good news that God loves them too. This philosophy, and this love, and these feelings, were to take over my own life. I was to be caught up in that same world of giving everything I had and everything I owned to the high-school kids of this country.

*   *   *

As I hit the brakes and began to slide off the highway, the lights of a small town brought me back to reality. Again the radio announcers were describing the devastation caused by hurricane Celia. My mind continued to run full speed, anxiety mixed with hurt, reflecting on mistakes I had made in my marriage and past mistakes with the kids. I guess that my poor beginning in life brought me to where I was, and I wondered whether after this trip home, I would even finish this life. A couple of times I almost flipped the car. I noticed that the gas tank was getting low as I turned onto 90 and headed for Hondo, the gas pedal still to the floorboard. In my mind and in my heart I felt that something terrible had already happened to Carolyn. Of course guilt and contributed fault plagued my mind.

5
Jump, Frog, Jump

It's always been hard for me to make the right decision at the right time. Deciding to go to college was extremely difficult. I knew I wanted to be involved in Young Life or some other area in order to work with teenagers in this country. Even those moments there in Colorado, during great peace, quiet, and study, I knew that somehow I had to get back to school. I felt that I wanted an education, and in some ways I felt that I was ready for it now. I enrolled that fall in Bryan University in Dayton, Tennessee. I lasted three weeks — not because of school, but because of me! One morning I knocked a kid across the bed into the wall because I still had a bad habit of hitting people. In a moment of anger I had released a blow that sent this kid to the floor. So I left Bryan, hitchhiked back to Colorado, back to another year of growing and studying.

Sooner or later, I thought, it's got to get better. And I guess that's what the next year was for me. I needed more time to find out who I was and to develop some good habits in my life. Things got a little better as the selfishness started going away. For the first time in my life I began to get "outside" of myself and more "into" the lives of others. My entire life to this point had always centered around one person — me!

In a little town east of Colorado Springs, the principal of the high school wanted a Young Life club, and Jim Rayburn felt that I could lead it. With a friend of mine we started a small Young Life club in this rural area. I would go to Jim's Young Life club in Colorado Springs on Tuesday night to steal his messages, then give them at our little club. Within three or four weeks we were having as many as thirty-five kids. Some had dropped out of school, but they

began to come to Young Life. I had a great year
ministering to those kids. God affirmed me so
many times as I tried to relate his love. I recall
one night a little girl stood up and said: "Because you've been coming to my high school,
and talking to me and my friends about Jesus
Christ, I've become a Christian." I'll never
forget the feeling I had that night.

That beautiful little girl was my first con-
vert, and I remember my excitement driving
back to Colorado Springs afterward . . . and my
prayer: "Lord! Thank you for that girl tonight.
As a result of this miracle, this is the kind of life
I want to continue to live. I want to give to
people. I want to be a witness to young people
for you and see them come to you and come to
know your love because I care enough to go to
them. I'll be your person, and I'll go where you
want me to go, and I'll do what you want me to
do."

What I didn't realize was that later events
in my life would bring me to the point when
I would want to break and renege on that
agreement and not be bound by those
words of prayer. There would be times when
I wouldn't want to do what he wanted me to
do, didn't want to be what he wanted me to be.
I would want to be somebody else, loud and

clear. I didn't want to be what he had made me. I wanted to run away from the commitment of giving my life to others whom he loved. Somehow in those moments of despair, he knew just how far he could push me. He knew exactly when to say, "I love you!"

*   *   *

The car radio brought me to my wits again, and I heard the report — nine deaths already in the hurricane. The information sounded a bit more authentic, and the broadcaster's tone was carrying a little more authority. By now the army had moved in and declared martial law in Corpus, sealing off the streets because of looting. There was no power or water. They were asking that no one attempt to come into the city or into the surrounding communities because all were closed off.

At this point it didn't even register with me that I would have any trouble getting into Corpus or to home. Celia had moved out of the area and was going across South Texas, heading toward Laredo and Mexico. I could see the large clouds building up off to the south of me as I drove U.S. 90 toward Hondo at a still-reckless speed, passing the few cars which were on the highway and hoping that no trooper would get anywhere close to me.

I was very concerned about friends in Corpus, our Young Life house at Port Aransas where there were sixty-five kids living for the summer. I tried to concentrate on our own home in Portland and on Carolyn, but the darkness of the highway and the lights reflecting off the concrete, the sing-song thumping of the tires against the road, lulled me back into a thought I'd had most of my early life: You're a nobody, and there's no sense in your trying to be anybody or anything.

*   *   *

As much as I had wanted to live my life for God and be involved with people — and even though I had tried many times to tell him I would try to be his person — it was only after that first experience as a leader that I began to come to terms with the many times I had wanted to break that promise. There had been great moments of doubt and frustration in my life, moments of loneliness and despair. One of the things that I had learned to do was to get the most out of every little bit of club experience in that small community in Colorado, and I grew in my ability to give. Yet I ended up destroying that club one night because a kid saw fit to ridicule me. He made fun of me, and afterwards I was so blasted angry and disturbed that I invited him out in the backyard and properly knocked the hell out of him. In one moment of immaturity and madness, which had been the credentials of most of my life, I ruined what I had spent a year putting together. One week later as we drove back for our final club with Bob Mitchell and the summer staff from Star Ranch, we planned a little party for the kids. Only seven or eight showed up, and we were justly challenged by every other kid in that town either to get out or they would run us out. In some ways we were lucky to escape with our lives, for those youngsters chased us half way from Payton to Colorado Springs.

All during that summer I wrestled with my insecurities. How could a person go from love to anger, to hate, in a matter of minutes? I had destroyed something that had taken a year to build. In such moments God began speaking to me about getting serious about school and growing up, finding out who I was, and accepting what I'd found.

Toward the end of the summer, a busload of kids from First Baptist Church, Shelby, North

Carolina, arrived at Star Ranch for camp week. One of their chaperons was a mild-voiced teacher of Greek and Bible at Gardner-Webb, a small Baptist junior college in North Carolina. During the week he and I had some talks and began to share feelings. I expressed a desire to return to school and my dreadful fear of failing. He shared his feelings with me, telling me that after watching me closely, he wanted me to come to Gardner-Webb Junior College. "I'll take care of the complete costs. I know you like to play football, and we have a good football team. I'll help you study, and I'll aid you in choosing the right courses, for we need your influence on our college campus." I agreed to go to Gardner-Webb that fall of 1949.

That was the first big event of that summer. The second one was a confrontation between Jim Rayburn and me. We had some pretty sticky encounters since he was a strong-willed, stubborn man and I, a very insecure, stubborn kid. We had a run-in about something, even though I had been praying for maturity and growth in our relationship. This time, Jim's beautiful wife, Maxine, was involved; and I had not wanted to apologize to him for giving him a hard time. But since I realized how much this man loved me and had done for me, I asked

God to give me the courage to go to him and tell him I was sorry for my poor attitude, for what I had done, and to tell him that I loved him.

I walked up to the front porch of the ranchhouse where Jim and Maxine were sitting, relaxing. For the first time in my life, "emotional me" had the ability to verbalize my inner feelings, which began to pour out. The happiest instant of my life was when I looked at those two dear people and said unabashedly: "For the first time, I'm prepared to tell you I'm sorry if I've hurt you; forgive me, for I love you both." Of course new feelings emerged with that confession, and the healing process that began was accompanied by a renewed sense of well-being. Now I was no longer afraid to admit that I was wrong; now I could ask forgiveness. To admit a mistake was a great step, a step of growth; an important step that would later make me at times almost completely unafraid of my feelings. Later I would retain the ability to express to people that I loved them, cared for them, and wanted to be involved in their lives. This too became the dominant factor in my life as I related Jesus Christ to the kids that I worked with and loved.

I also learned a great deal that summer about interacting with young people. A particularly tough bunch of kids came to the ranch from one of our clubs in Southern California. I suppose the busride had been wild; one of them had even stabbed another member of this group in a restroom in Santa Fe. They were tough, smartalecky kids away from home, but we were ready for them when they arrived.

They came with the most negative attitudes of any kids that had ever come to camp. They had decided far in advance that they weren't going to like it, were not going to participate, and they just intended to wipe out the week. The first two days was pure hell. I remember times when I just wanted to knock the daylights out of them. For some reason, I didn't. We just kept trying to love and understand them, and to communicate to them that we loved them and cared for them. Bob Mitchell and I even prayed together that something good would happen to those kids. We had some fine young people on our staff at that time, and eventually these big-mouth, smartalecks got around to challenging that staff of Christians to a football game. "Well," they said, "we'll take those fancy Christians and bust them up a little."

Before the game all the kids were down on the field, for it was to be the match of the year since those tough kids wanted to put it to us, and put it to us hard. I knew we had to get them first. They needed to learn that Christians had feelings too and that Christians also could play tough, be tough if necessary. Also, we wanted to impress upon them that Christianity took much more than they had imagined. We were in one corner of the field — the work crew and staff — and we asked a little prayer before the football game. One of the staff prayed the funniest yet most appropriate prayer I'd ever heard: "You know, God, you know us and you know these other guys. Help us to hit these fellows and hit them hard, harder than we've ever hit anybody before. But help us to hit them with love."

It was a fun afternoon. One thing those toughies didn't know was that we had two or three high-school all-staters and one all-American high-school football player working on our crew. We could do just about anything we wanted with that game. They kicked off the ball to us. I was playing tailback, and as the ball approached me, I grabbed it and ran straight up the middle of the field without even being touched. I looked back as I neared the goal, and every guy on the California team was lying prone on the ground. Our guys had chopped them down like they were tomato plants. We had given them the worst beating they had *had* in a long time. We finally quit after three quarters at a score of 36-0. We had to take two of them with possible injuries to the hospital.

About midway in that game, I had started feeling sorry for those kids. They were so much like me when I was growing up, always trying to prove something to somebody. I guess maybe I was just trying to prove something to myself — that I was a tough man, so look out! That night the meeting was a success, and as Jim Rayburn spoke, you could sense that the attitudes of all those kids had changed toward Christians per se. One youngster, president of his high-school class in California, stood up and announced that he had never thought much of Christianity, but that today he learned how Christians could live and pray.

It was a great week. Almost all the kids ended up loving us as we loved them. Many of them entrusted their lives to Jesus Christ. It is interesting how God used a football game to break open kids to his love. But he chooses to do this; he chooses to do it his way, and he chose a bunch of funny-looking older guys like us to play, to break down the barriers of some high-school kids who needed to learn of his love and methods.

That fall, as I left the Colorado ranch and headed for Shelby, North Carolina, I was filled with misgivings about the next two years. Could Frog the Failure make it as a college student?

A New 6
Pad

Gardner-Webb Junior College was the backdrop of a carefree, beautiful two years. I played football under a tremendous coach and became one of the leading students on campus. During those two years, I began to develop good study habits that were desperately needed. I wrote to a friend in Memphis, telling him that for the first time in my life I was *enjoying* studying. I scheduled all my classes in the morning in order to devote afternoons to study, lunch, and football practice. At night I studied more; I carried some hard courses. I was making 60 in English and 90 in Greek . . . guess I should have been a Greek!

Never before had I realized or dreamed how it felt to experiment with ideas, to swirl them around in my head, to join rap sessions in the dorm with other guys. New doors had been opened to me for researching, and thresholds were crossed intellectually. At this stage of my development I came to love two tremendous girls — a new, different experience for me. They were neat girls, and we became very warm friends. I became involved with the kids in Shelby Young Life club in a positive manner — a club of about two hundred kids. I helped Mr. Harris, who was also pastor of the First Baptist Church, run the club, and together we saw a good many changes in the lives of many of those kids. Today one of those boys is a regional director of Young Life. He was an outstanding basketball player in those days, and it was great being around to watch him as a spectator might — to observe the changes in his life and in the lives of other kids I was close to. That commitment I had made earlier — of giving my life to high-school kids if that was what God wanted — began to blossom and bear fruit.

Although my books, tuition, and fees were paid, I didn't have a lot of spare money. But Mr. and Mrs. Harris were great people when it came to helping me. I used their cars and lived in their home on weekends.

Upon graduation, I received some offers to play football. Some of the smaller colleges in both North and South Carolina offered scholarships, but I did not feel that athletics was what I wanted to devote my time to. Dick Langford, the Young Life director at Knoxville, was a warm, sincere man who loved people. He had many things going in Knoxville for Young Life, and he needed some college students to assist him. He asked me to live in his home, to go to the University of Tennessee, and to start a new club with him.

Ever since I was a dirty-faced little kid I had heard of the University of Tennessee — its great powerhouse football teams and its academic reputation. I guess I was thinking about playing football for them even then. But I knew that dream was impossible, for they were national champs in '50 — a great football team under the gun of General Neyland. "Digger," as we called Dick Langford, and I spent a day together just praying over it. I sent in my registration forms, and much to my amazement,

I was accepted for the fall of 1951. Boy, the next two years were ones of continual growth for me. For one thing, I met Carolyn . . .

*   *   *

Just as that thought hit my mind, the lights of Hondo came into view, the rain solidly pelting my windshield. At that instant I became aware of the radio and heard how the end of the hurricane was moving into south San Antonio, Pleasanton, Hondo, and then cutting a path across to Mexico. I pulled into a nearby service station, asked that they please hurry to "fill'er up" and check the oil, which they did. I wasn't there but a couple of minutes when I leaped back into my car and pushed my foot to the floorboard. I smiled as I spied that funny familiar sign as I sped into and out of Hondo: "This is God's country . . . so don't drive through it like hell!" I certainly had thrown caution to the wind.

The news reports continued to be increasingly disturbing. Now I was concerned about the South Texas communities that were completely sealed off to outsiders. There were reports of flooding caused by the continuous heavy rains. Also there was a possibility — and a good one — that I would not even get into Portland to find Carolyn, once I hit that first roadblock.

Carolyn was now continually on my mind, and I found myself reminiscing about those two years at the University of Tennessee where we had met.

7
The Frog Meets the Princess

When I first enrolled at the university, I had no idea I was to meet the beautiful, bright, talented woman who was to become my wife and companion. The switch from junior college to the University of Tennessee caused me to suffer real cultural shock, moving from a small campus to a large one, living in a dorm, not having enough money to pay for cafeteria fees, and not knowing where the next meal was to come from. The Langfords, with whom I lived, helped me much even though they didn't have a lot. It was joyful living in their beautiful home with their two fine children. They both had such a beneficial influence on my life at that time. There was much happiness and laughter between us; many funny things were discussed at the table.

Once again I was studying; and once again, failing. My first two courses at the university were chemistry and a very difficult math course, and with that math course came that unbearable feeling of failure. At this stage of my life I wasn't at all free to fail. But then I never had felt free to fail in the past; and in the future I would never feel free to fail, either. That relentless masculine image-monster I had created demanded that all men succeed, and if you didn't succeed, you were not a man. This fallacy had dominated me all of my life, and now it hurt.

One of the first things I got into was starting a Young Life club at Fulton High School. It was a tough school but had some fine kids that I had gotten involved with. So many of those kids have done well since then — kids who learned to open their hearts and lives to Jesus Christ through that club and our relationship. Two of them are now with Young Life (one a divisional director and the other a top man in the leadership echelon of Young Life). That very first night with the club, seventy-five kids jammed into a little old house, including half the football team, the cheerleaders, and prominent leaders of the school. Many of the student body showed up for the session. I saw so much of myself in the faces of some of those youngsters that night. We had such fun identifying with each other. It turned out to be a fine club, which I enjoyed leading for two years. Wonderful things happened to some of those young people. Once again I felt affirmation from God that I was where I was supposed to be, doing what I was meant to do.

During these two years I met Carolyn and her sisters, Judy and Inabelle. They had become involved as Christians in Young Life in Knoxville. We had gotten to be friends, and I recall one Sunday morning going to church and meeting Carolyn there at the service. She struck me as being very aloof and indifferent, but strikingly beautiful. I am sure that I impressed her as a jerk, an egotist mainly concerned with himself and what he did. I often came through to people that way. She wasn't impressed with me, and I don't recall being too impressed with her. Nothing clicked until Christmas. I had gone home to work at the local post office to earn some money with which to go back to college. Carolyn and one of her sisters had a bitter argument over something pretty insignificant, and for some reason when she got to Memphis, where she had gone to college at Memphis State, she called me. We had lunch downtown and spent some time talking over our situations. That night we had a date, and that was the beginning of our relationship. I decided I liked what I saw!

In one day Carolyn and I learned about each other. We enjoyed being together! She was a warm person, searching for life and someone to love, and she was afraid. A bright girl, graduating from college at twenty-one, she had already suffered disappointments in her life. We had fun together that week in Memphis, dating and meeting some old friends. Then we rode back to Knoxville on the train together. During that spring we began to date more frequently. We had so many good times talking for hours about life and the things we both wanted from it. In some ways we were extreme opposites. She was, and is, a bright woman with tremendous drive. To be successful and get all the things she never had while she was growing up was important to her. For me, I wanted the relationships and accomplishments that God wanted of me, more than anything material. Carolyn and I began to spend more time together, being close. She helped in the Young Life club; we just paired up as a team. During that spring I knew I was falling in love with Carolyn; yet I was afraid we might clash, that she might not want me or the things I wanted.

Sometime between Christmas and Easter that year — Carolyn doesn't know when and I don't know when — just through the process of talking and being together, loving each other, she gave her life to Christ. We were in Memphis at Eastertime, and she stayed with a friend while I stayed with my family. We began to learn to love each other and appreciate our compatibility. I was gradually starting to be afraid of the love that had developed and now existed between us. I had to confess one Sunday afternoon that I was afraid, and for some stupid reason I told her that I was not sure whether I loved her. Seeing her cry for the first time during our courtship was a moment in my life when I realized that the only persons you can really hurt are the ones you love, and only they can hurt you. That was the first of many times I was to hurt Carolyn, and I was to hurt her very much.

In my stumbling, bumbling way of doing

things, I hurt a lot of people. Hurt them when I didn't even know it. I guess it was the thing that I didn't want to do but never learned to avoid. Acquiring the refinements of life did not come easy — and not at all — until much later on. The social graces were a mystery. In some ways I never was a phony until I became a Christian. I saw Christian people knowingly hurt others and enjoying it for the most part, and they did it in the name of Christianity. That's been a hard one for me to understand. When God talks about kindness and love, why do we often set out deliberately to hurt one another?

That summer after my junior year at the university, Carolyn and I decided to work in Memphis so that we could spend our time together. I'd spent no time with my parents since I graduated from high school. Carolyn stayed with an aunt in Memphis and got a job immediately. I found a job, and we spent lots of time together as we planned.

We never talked much of getting married or any definite moves like that. We both realized that we wanted each other, but I never once asked her if she would marry me. I simply said to her one fine day, "Why don't we go down and pick out a ring 'cause I feel like buying a present for my wife." I'm not sure how much I prayed about our union although I'm sure I did. I know that I wanted the marriage if that was what God wanted for me. We picked out rings and became engaged. It was a grand summer spent working and playing together. We went to the lakes in Mississippi and played in the sun, laughed and talked, and loved each other. Some of those days of that summer were the happiest of my life. There were days when I didn't sense much responsibility or much concern; all I wanted was to be with Carolyn and get to know her better — and enjoy our mutual and consuming love.

We went back to the University of Tennessee for my senior year. A long engagement followed. We learned so much about each other during that time. One night we were talking and getting in a few smacks when I said something that made her mad, so mad that she took her ring and threw it out the car window; we almost never found it. We wound up laughing and very relieved. So many funny things like that happened.

Both of us were intensely aware of the love of God in our hearts; we couldn't separate his love from ours for each other. I guess you can't separate the guts of a man from the spirit of God. On the inside, I seem to be the way God probably created me from my conception. I've seen Christians split their feelings about themselves and about the world they live in, all the while keeping him underneath as they try to express and isolate their "spiritual feelings." Is this why so many Christians are filled with guilt and anxiety? So many Christians have nervous breakdowns and psychological problems. Much of it must stem from their inability to express exactly how they feel.

Carolyn and I began to relate to each other very well. I wanted her and loved her dearly. My senior year at the university was fun, for we had made it so. The spring of that year brought the final decision to the surface. The initial commitment which I had made to God to go where he wanted me to go and do as he wanted me to do convinced me that Carolyn was to be part of that arrangement. I intended to carry through my pledge to him no matter the cost. I agreed to come on the Young Life staff and move to Denver, Colorado, as area director for Young Life. That summer I had to go to school, so we planned our wedding for the end of the term . . . and had fun doing it. Neither of us had any money. Carolyn had bought a car while she was teaching. I graduated from the university on August 22, 1953, and Carolyn and I were married two days later. It was a delightful wedding. Some of the kids from Young Life came along with some of our best friends. I never knew until that night what it was to give yourself to another person without qualms; I'd never done that before. I was so selfish and self-centered and so impressed with who I was, how important I was. I didn't even know that this was a front and that realistically none of it was true.

8

The Frog
Takes the
Princess
Away

The next fourteen years were to be struggling and fighting ones. Perhaps I sensed this as we got into our car and left Knoxville; for I wondered what I had just done. I had *given* myself to another person. Doubts flooded my mind. That week I had not sensed the fine hand of God as I had previously.

I graduated from the university without any money. My mom and dad came for the graduation ceremony and stayed on for the wedding that followed. Dad, who had very little money, slipped me some bills. That Sunday night before we were married, I preached at the small Presbyterian church nearby. I remember this sweet little old lady coming up and telling me: "Because of what you have meant to the kids in Knoxville and because of what you mean to our church . . ." as she slipped something into my hand, telling me it was "a token, not much, but it shows my love for you." Later, outside, when I opened my hand to see the "token," I found five brand-new twenty-dollar bills. Tears flowed freely — as they have so often in my life — for once again I was aware that God was going to uphold his end of our agreement — he was going to take care of me.

My job with Young Life did not provide us enough to live on. Even though Carolyn didn't have a job in Denver, we left undaunted, on our four-day honeymoon, driving to Colorado. They were four of the funniest days one could ever imagine. One of the most hilarious incidents occurred in Stuckey, Kansas, at a dry-county Methodist youth rally, where I had accepted a speaking engagement for a much-needed fifty-dollar speaker's fee. The county fair was going on so there was "no room at the inn," so to speak. I strolled up to a three-story hotel which looked rather nice on the outside although a bit run-down. I went in, asked the desk clerk if he had a room, and after he said yes, he had one left, told him we would take it. I never had traveled much, so I didn't bother to ask if it had a bathroom. We discovered that although we had a room to sleep in, we had to share the johns and showers with everyone else on that floor. I was disappointed, to say the least, and I saw the disappointment in Carolyn's eyes and face as we walked into that room together. But I had disappointed her at other times during the year and a half we had gone together, so she was not overcome by this relic of a hotel. We put down our suitcases, sat on the edge of the bed, and bang, it fell through. Deciding a shower would make us feel better, we headed for it, only to discover it had no locks on the door; so we held the door for each other while we took our showers. It wasn't funny then, but to both of us now, in retrospect, it is one of those experiences we shall never forget.

As Carolyn and I drove into Denver after being married only four days and knowing only one or two people there, I felt scared. With the fear of a small child, loneliness and hurt set in. I felt I had once again undertaken something that was too big; once again I was attempting to overachieve. As we drove over the top of a hill and looked down upon that huge, beautiful, lighted city surrounded by mountains — home for a million people — I remember thinking with a sick feeling that here, God, was my parish! That was to be the first of many times I have pleaded: "God, forget it! The deal's off! There is no way I can do the things you want of me." Only because of my compulsion, my drive to prove I was a man, the tremendous drive to be successful because no one in my family had been up until that time, was I able to overcome the fear that I might eventually fail.

I pushed myself twelve, thirteen hours a day, seven days a week in that community, trying to reach as many kids as I possibly could. Time and again I was reassured and fascinated by the way God took care of us. For instance, Carolyn needed a job. We walked into the school superintendent's office, and she was immediately hired to replace a girl who had just quit her job. It seemed to be God's way of saying that *this* was what he wanted — I came to believe that!

We settled down to enjoy life in Denver. Some weekends we'd go to the mountains, where I began to learn to ski. The ski slope became one of the places where I could find some peace with relaxation. I was still an extremely selfish human being, but I hid my self-interest under the cloak of what God wanted me to be and do in his name. I was learning to do more things for Carolyn, however; she was coming more frequently into my sphere of thinking, and I was devoting more effort into being a husband. But one weekend is still vivid in my memory; I learned a few hard facts about myself and my hangups. I thought nothing of scheduling a weekend away from Carolyn and not saying a word to her about it. I wouldn't even bother to tell her that I was going to be out of town all weekend speaking at a camp someplace until she found me packing my suitcase to leave. I crushed her like this from time to time; not intentionally, and not because I didn't love her — it was just this stupid compulsion to win the world for God on my own. There was just nobody else in Denver doing anything for Jesus but me. And I was thoroughly convinced if I didn't get out there and get it done, it just might not ever get done.

I lived at that level for seven years in Denver. We had vibrant work going and good things happening in the lives of kids. Again I was building solid relationships with kids and with people in the community. I met Rowland

Hetrick, and he remains to this day one of my dearest friends. We developed a real man-to-man relationship, and he had a great influence over me during those days. In his quiet deep way he would often say to me, at times when I was considering quitting this time-and-energy consuming career I had chosen: "You know, to be able to do what you do and relate Christ to kids and people . . . why I'd give my business and all my money to be able to do that the way you do." That thought was to grow on me, slowly becoming a dominating thought in my life. I was to become a people-person, mostly because I needed people! I didn't fully accept that need then, but I needed people very much and still do. This great need instinctively filled my days, but there came a frustrating point because I always wanted to be where the action was.

We loved Denver; and our two children, Cathy and Scott, were born there. Today Cathy is a beautiful, sensitive girl and Scott, a great little guy. But as usual, I wasn't at Carolyn's side when either of them was born. Crucial times in our lives always found me somewhere else doing something or other for someone other than my own family. The adage "charity begins at home" certainly wasn't built into my philosophy.

In the spring of 1960, we were asked to move to Oklahoma City. While we wrestled with the decision about whether or not to go, we asked aloud what we ought to do as family. The commitment with God that I would work where he wanted and be his kind of person prevailed. I guess the internal battles with this decision became so profound that I tried covering them up. Instead of everything becoming good, tremendous, and loving in the Christian life, I bound myself up in a continuous struggle, masquerading under the disguise of who I was, what I wanted out of life, why I had never found the peace that God talked about. Ninety percent of my life I stayed so torn up on the inside that I hardly ever slept beyond four or five hours per night. Those hours of confrontation with myself and God were spent bargaining with God that if I went to Oklahoma City he would somehow take care of me. So . . . we moved.

*   *   *

The rain was now coming down in torrents, furiously pelting the car. As I began driving through the hurricane from Hondo to Pleasanton, the wind was blowing like mad, but I was still driving at top speed. Three times that wind turned my car completely around as I sped on. Reflections on our life together brought tears to my eyes as I prayed to God not to let anything happen to Carolyn. As I headed for home, I wondered: Would I make it? Had Carolyn made it?

9
Frog Builds Big Pond

One of the big regrets in my life and the one thing I still feel most guilty about today is that I left the rearing of our children pretty much up to Carolyn. We never were much of a family unit since I was usually gone, out running around doing God's work. It wasn't until later on that I began to see the need Carolyn and the kids had for my love. I did love them all and wanted for them the things I never had: love, peace, and joy. I wanted the kids to grow up knowing themselves better, to know Christ and love him. I didn't want them to go through the hurt, the humiliation, and other crazy things I experienced during my early days. They were two neat kids, and I had lots of fun playing with them. Carolyn worked so hard in order to provide them things the two of us never had. She was an unbelievably good mother. In her determination to be an excellent mother, she had a profound influence on their lives.

The move to Oklahoma City was disturbing. We found ourselves in a cautious situation, where the major backers of Young Life were members of the most outstanding power structure of the community. Good-looking, smart, wealthy, sharp young Christian businessmen and women caught us up in their kind of world. A lot of things began to materialize in my ministries with them. It was there, in the beginning of 1960, I realized that most of the ability to reach the core of the community was through its children. By having a successful program of ministries with the children of the community, we could get involved with their parents. With this in mind, I poured myself into the lives of those kids as I'd never done before. Their clubs began to explode, sending bursts of leadership upon the local high-school scene. Within a few years we had gone from a mere four clubs to an active eleven. The Putnam City club emerged as the largest Young Life club in the United States, and for five years averaged between four and five hundred kids every week. I loved that club for the success it was, and for me it was the outstanding club in the entire Young Life organization.

In many ways, Young Life blew Oklahoma City wide open, but I paid a price doing it. I sacrificed my family and my health. Along the way, I built splendid relationships with adults and other people's kids; and we began to raise the money that made Young Life possible. At one time we were in every high school in Oklahoma City except one. Then in the middle of an ever-increasing amount of professional activity and responsibility, I felt a strong urge to go back to school. I longed to know more about myself: what made me tick and who I was. So I took a few hours of psychology here and there. Finally I persuaded Young Life to give me seven months' leave in order to finish my master's degree. How hard I worked . . . how I learned to love study . . . how much I learned about my own intellectual structure.

I drove myself so hard that spring and summer that I almost lost my identity in the process. I struggled long and hard with problems, never thinking much about what I believed or why I believed as I did. As I began to work out some of these problems, life became meaningful to me. While going to school to examine my insides, I fashioned a friendship with a man whom I didn't know well then — and he didn't know me either — but we struck chords in each other's lives. This man, Bill Yinger, was in the oil business in Oklahoma City, and as a practicing Christian, he was struggling with all the baloney that goes on in the business world. He couldn't buy the concept that Christians had few problems as they faced daily living, that all they had to do was take it easy with Jesus and then peace, quiet, and tranquility would fill their hearts and lives. He couldn't buy that, and yet he wanted to be God's person amid the hordes of humanity.

In those days the struggles in my own life began to rise to a precarious peak. Carolyn and I were having a difficult time living together. I had hurt her so much. I had not been a thoughtful husband or father to my children. I was a man who existed in a shell trying to make enough money so we could live, and I was doing a very poor job of it. Guilt, resentment, and hatred welled up within me. The resulting hard feelings I developed became almost insurmountable.

Keith Miller, a partner of Bill Yinger in the oil business in Oklahoma City, was a breath of fresh air in those days. We would eat lunch and talk together for hours. He would relate his troubles to me so I could begin to recognize similar ones in my own life. More than anything in this world I wished to be a real person. I didn't want to be a phony, but I was so phony it was ludicrous. I didn't want to be compulsive. I sensed that I wasn't God's man sent to save the world, and I knew in my heart that I was just another being that God loved, cared for, and wanted to relate himself to in turn, so that I might relate to others. We had both been battling so hard with this; thus we found it necessary to sit and talk it through, hopefully honest and open about our feelings. This exchange was a whole new concept for me because I had never before expressed my personal feelings to anyone ... not even to Carolyn. Keith and I were pretty close in those days. I respect him as one of the most influential men in the Christian world today. Perhaps because of his own struggles, he too ended up going back to graduate school.

After I graduated with my master's, I found I had learned a great deal about myself in the process. I had struggled with some of the insidious problems in my own life, including my relationship with Carolyn. I was working hard, trying to be real. One Thanksgiving as I walked out the door at home on the way to speak at a camp some place, Carolyn said to me: "Do you know, or do you even care, that from the middle of September until today, you have not been home one night?" She was right. I had been so caught up in who I was that I was crushing her and our children.

10
Frog Releases Princess

The following summer was a real turning point for us. Our struggles continued, and Carolyn enrolled in graduate school. We took a vacation in Florida for three weeks which turned out to be a happy time with the children. We walked on the beach at Daytona, played in the surf, and loved each other like never before. I began to sense the phoniness, the dishonesty, and the rest of the hypocrisy I was presenting. These things began to come to the surface as we rested and relaxed. Slowly I began to realize one of the things I had to do — "release Carolyn." I had to let her be herself. I had to quit dominating her entire life. I just had to turn her loose. Whatever she wanted had to be what I wanted.

I remember one morning, three or four o'clock, down on the beach. I tried to share with her and explain to her that I didn't want to control her life anymore, that I was setting her free. If she didn't want to live with me, she was free to leave. I told her I loved her very much and needed her, wanted her — that she could take the kids or that I would take the kids. She was free to go to graduate school even though I had not really wanted her to; she was now free to go to work. I no longer wanted to dominate her life or manipulate her. That was a freeing experience. I let Carolyn go, emotionally, and when it was over, I remember how very much love I felt for her — more than ever before. I think this was the first really honest love I had shown her in our relationship.

I left Carolyn, Cathy, and Scott with Carolyn's mother and drove back to Oklahoma City — about the happiest I had ever been in my life. I felt some healing and some health in our relationship. I was beginning to feel good about who I was, and I made some plans to change my life. And, I did! Carolyn stayed with her mother for a couple of weeks while I went to Laity Lodge, where Keith Miller was a director. I was then to go to Colorado for a college-prep camp. That trip back to Oklahoma City was spent driving and praying. I didn't realize it then, but the next two weeks were going to become the second most significant two in my life.

I spent a few days in Oklahoma City working in my office, getting some things together for fall. I had some strange feelings about all that had taken place. I wondered if I meant what I had said to Carolyn, that she was free! One morning I prayed: "Oh, God, please don't let her leave." I had crushed her spirit, and I wanted her to be as free as she wanted to be again. When I met her, she was such a vivacious and beautiful person, and in a lot of ways I changed all that. I had made her almost a nothing because everything around my house had to be built and geared around me — what I did, who I was, and where I was going.

As I got in my car to drive to Leakey, Texas, to Laity Lodge, I began to sense my feelings of anger, hostility, and depression. These feelings were not new to me, mostly because of how phony I had been in the past. I could see the tears in Carolyn's eyes when I told her she was free. What she really wanted was me. I had never given her what she wanted, and that was someone who really loved her — me. I knew in those hours that what I had said to Carolyn was going to be difficult to abide by, but I felt good about having said it.

I felt that by freeing her I had improved our relationship. But it was too late — for me and for her. On the way to Leaky, I crashed and burned emotionally like I'd never crashed in my life. By the time I reached Abilene, I was so disturbed I registered in a motel, stretched across a bed, and cried for hours. I begged God to take me and destroy me. I had flashbacks of how phony I was, how dishonest I had been most of my life. All the time I was ministering to people I was telling them how beautiful Christ was — and he *was* — that he could come into their lives and do things for them in some strange way. Yet I had never grasped this at a feeling level in my own life. I was so caught up with *me* that when I was introduced to someone, if that person didn't say, "Oh, yeah, I know you. I've heard of you, Frog Sullivan. Everybody has heard of you!" — if that person didn't relate to me, inside of me I just looked at him standoffishly and thought: "I wonder what kind of a bum he is, spending most of his life and not having heard of the great Frog Sullivan?"

I came closer that night in the motel to destroying myself than ever before, even in the darkest corners of my past. I considered calling the local hospital, or calling Keith to come and get me. Finally I decided to take a walk to clear my mind. I walked and I cried my heart out. All the loneliness and hurt of my entire past rained down on me at one time, and in one moment I faced how phony and unreal I'd been. I remember the police stopped and picked me up. In broken words I told them who I was and where I was staying. They escorted me back to the motel, where I walked into my room alone, and falling upon the floor, felt my guts eating my life away. I wanted to die. Finally in the wee hours of the morning, God pulled me through and brought me to my senses. I attempted to verbalize to him the guilt, the frustration, and the feeling of being so phony and out of touch . . . all the games I had played — and thinking I was getting by! I confessed I had used people, especially Carolyn. The whole experience proved very disturbing, but in the next two days it was to become the seeding of a new person. I simply had never accepted myself or my honest feelings. I had never accepted my insights, and in some ways I had never deeply accepted God. I was the "Great Pretender"; I had only *pretended* to accept his life for me. After I confessed all this to him, I felt a kind of peace that I'd never before experienced.

I drove into Laity Lodge, and when Keith saw me, he knew all hell was breaking loose. Just by looking at me (he had just finished writing *The Taste of New Wine*) he *knew* for he had struggled through some of the same things I had. I am not sure that either of us went to bed that weekend, and as I began to relate to him my feelings of loneliness and phoniness, I just wanted to junk the whole thing. A couple of months later, a close friend in Oklahoma City, another man who had been brutally frank with me, said: "Frog, I've been trying to tell you all along that you weren't a Christian. So now you've become one!" I sometimes wonder if that evaluation wasn't the truth. My rich new encounter with God began to set the stage for what was going to happen to Carolyn and me in the next years. I would need all the strength and insight I had found during those moments to carry me through to being the kind of person God was going to start shaping inside my skin.

*   *   *

The radio brought me back to my senses as I came into Pleasanton, Texas, flaring through the rain at the fuzzy lights of that little town, the wind practically blowing me off the highway. I pulled into an Exxon station to fill up for the next leg. The station attendant told me how bad it was in Corpus and how I'd not get into the city because it had been sealed off. My frustration and anxiety level began to go crazy again. Where is Carolyn, I wondered? How is she? And how could she forgive me for this one? I'd really blown it again. I felt the fear, the hurt, the anger, and the frustration of it all like chunks of debris hitting me in the chest.

As I sped out of that station in Pleasanton and headed for Corpus, depression struck me full-force. I doubted seriously if Carolyn was alive. If she was, I imagined she was angry since there I was, off working with somebody else's kids while she had to take this disastrous blow by herself. I died a million deaths wondering if maybe my life wasn't finished, that if this indeed was not the end for Carolyn and me, for our family. My mind drifted back to other moments of my life when I had been the most desperate . . .

11
Frog Can't Receive

The summer after I received my master's degree, Carolyn received hers. She wanted to be a professional counselor at the time. We had tried unsuccessfully to revamp our lives that year; and I endeavored to spend more time at home and be more real with her. I believed our love was growing through the devotion of additional time to her. I was also devoting more time to my kids, but my efforts seemed much too late. That year I watched, as Carolyn slowly deteriorated, pulling herself into a shell. One morning I woke up and looked over beside our bed to find her sitting there glassy-eyed, hurt, staring. That afternoon I admitted her to the psychiatric ward in a local hospital for thirty-six days. I did not know then, but the doctor told me later, that Carolyn was totally exhausted, both emotionally and mentally, and that the reason he was admitting her to the hospital was so that she could have rest and he could see her every day. This scared me to death!

I had been taught all my life that Christians do not have problems and that if we had really been trusting God, Carolyn would not be in this physical condition. I believe that I had been led wrongly to think that somehow because your life is open to God that you are not vulnerable to emotional problems. I believe now that the Christian is actually more vulnerable because he is struggling with his relationship to church and his relationship to his loved ones and the outside world all at the same time. I knew these were horrible moments of confinement for Carolyn, and I don't know yet all the feelings that she suffered that day. They were the worst few hours of my life.

When they put her in those rooms and I heard the doors lock as I walked away, something soft died within me. The severity of the

situation hit me: I felt totally responsible for
how Carolyn was and what had happened to
her; because of me she had lost control of
herself; she was deeply wounded. She had
been through enough psychology courses to
know at what point she needed help, and I
wasn't the one to help her.

I drove home to tell Scott and Cathy that
their mom was going to be in the hospital for a
few days. Not knowing how long it was going to
be, or whether she was ever going to come out
cured, I took the children for a hamburger and
talked with them endlessly. I got them ready
for bed and continued to talk. I knew that night
that I was facing a crisis in my own life that
would either make me or ruin me. That afternoon I had gone to a friend's house and had
taken a fifth of whiskey of theirs home with me.
After I put those kids to bed and prayed with
them, my little Cathy saw me cry for the first
time in her life. She said: "Dad, I've never seen
you cry before." I think that night she learned
some things about her dad. That I was a man,
that I was human, that I was hurt, alone and
lonely.

I bathed, put on some pajamas, and headed
for the icebox to mix a drink. At that very
moment I think I acknowledged I was through

with God for good, through with the Christian life I'd known because I had given everything to him and had now ended up with nothing but a hurt, lonely, confused wife and a nest of problems. I was really angry, knowing once again that I had hurt Carolyn deeply. As I went to the refrigerator, the doorbell rang, and an unbelievably wonderful man, Jack Johnston, was standing in the doorway.

I had already prayed earlier that night, and in the middle of my prayer I told God that I didn't understand. I had kept my end of the bargain, but he had done this dastardly thing to me. I didn't even know where he was or what he wanted from me any longer. I had given him my life blood and my family, and now he was trying to destroy me. As Jack walked into the room, he grabbed me and hugged me tight for maybe ten or fifteen minutes, I don't remember. He hugged me so tight and with such strength of caring, that my anger, bitterness, and disappointment seemed transferred from my fragile soul to his very being. He never quoted verses, he never said everything was going to be all right; he just blessed me with a short prayer and walked out the door, carrying my hostilities into the night.

I didn't understand it then, and I don't

pretend to understand it now. I still don't understand what happened to Carolyn. But because of Jack, I was able to accept the situation. The love we received from Christians in the next few months was astounding, overwhelmingly beautiful. Meals were brought into our home for one solid month. People came to make up our beds, clean our house. I received money in envelopes through the mail from unknown sources to help with medical expenses that soared out of sight. Linda Rolfs, a great girl, who had met Christ in our Putnam City Young Life club, lived in our home the next two months, taking care of our kids, playing ball with them, loving them, and just doing everything for them imaginable. As I look back on that crisis, it was unbelievable the way our Christian community ministered to me and my family. It was a long struggle for Carolyn, and the psychiatrist reported it would be a lonely struggle as well for me since primarily this was her problem — only she could work through it.

I died so many times that year as I watched her seemingly endless struggle to put her life back together, to find some sense or meaning to it. I came to love her more in so many ways, realizing what a neat person she had always been and would hopefully be again. After some of the faulty early attempts, we tried once again to relate more and more of our feelings, with anger, love, and hostility spilling out to each other in order to deepen our relationship. But it was difficult to watch her struggle so much and not be able to help more, not be able to understand what she was shedding. Just my being there counted for what she needed most. It was a trying time for both of us. So many days during this period I found God adequate in meeting my needs. This was also a time of getting reacquainted with my children, staying at home longer, and being with them more often.

The thing that destroys a good many of us as Christians is our inability to relate to each other in a warm, honest, compassionate sort of way. Even with those to whom I was close, I failed in this endeavor. I was so busy being a "doing" Christian (Boy, that certainly was me!) that I'd forgotten what God called me to *be*. For so long I didn't know that a Christian was supposed to let someone love him; I thought that he was always supposed to be loving somebody else. I didn't think it was necessary to let anyone love me, including Carolyn. It seems that in the context of my Christian faith, you were adequate if you could love people; but you were considered inadequate if you let them love you.

Great things began to happen in my life when I found out how much I needed love from Carolyn and my children. I came to terms with how much I needed other Christians around me, and how much I wanted recognition with love from the high-school kids, and from the world God had made. I began to realize that God is the one who gives; and we are the ones who receive. I discovered giving love is not difficult for some of us; but for me, receiving love and letting people love me was one of the most trying things that I as a Christian had to learn. But these discoveries began to become working realities in my life. They began to release me from the fear of not being accepted. Intensive self-reevaluation helped me to love people whether they returned that love or not. I could love someone, and if that person wanted to reject me, he was free to do it without causing me lasting misgivings. It was my place and purpose to love and let it be.

As a result of these changes in my own personality, my relationship with the Young Life kids in Oklahoma City began to intensify. My awareness of the world and what was going on helped me become much more sensitive to people's needs and feelings — what they were, what they were looking for, what they wanted in their lives. What had begun to happen in my life was the breaking open of a new person, the shedding of old hang-ups, and the receiving of joy.

The Putnam City Young Life club had grown to be very large. We had so many tremendous kids coming to it, finding faith in the life of Jesus Christ. I can remember a couple who broke through to me at this time in a deep personal way. Many of those kids were tough, hard-nosed characters; but through a personal relationship with God — through me — a lot of them began to change from tough, dirty kids, into sweet, kind, loving individuals. This affirmed to me that the idea and practice of loving people and letting them love in return was what God really wanted of me, and maybe of a lot of "professional" Christians. I began to see that as Christians we had to do more than just love people in general and talk to them about Christ. The ultimate goal, of course, was to lead them to a personal faith. But the actual healing takes place when we become personally and thoroughly involved in the lives of other people, not only in the little things but in the big things as well. We love life, but we have to learn to laugh and let live and let others love us back.

Carolyn began to improve; so she came home sooner than the doctor had first thought. Slowly, we rebuilt our relationship with each other and with the kids. I guess it was then that I first began to try to reconstruct my whole life. I had quit doing as much traveling, speaking at weekend camps, and I had liked those activities, enjoyed the participation. My ego flourished with the identification that most kids made with Frog Sullivan. But now I had to think of Carolyn first; so I opened up to her and let her love me freely. This was extremely difficult since I was still living on the premise that if you needed someone, this meant you were inadequate unto yourself. But my new attitude began to do something constructive for our relationship. I realized how easy it is to say "I love you," and how reaffirming and renewing it is. I had always wondered if people really meant it when they said "I love you" to me. But I am no longer afraid to believe them or let them love me.

Giving and receiving love became equally important to me, though basically I knew only God could really give love. It is difficult for a person with a strong ego to admit that he needs, is starved for, love. Yes, I ultimately need love from God because God is the greatest person or concept I've run across in the world. He doesn't necessarily need consuming love from other human beings. It was hard for me to let people love me, but it was the beginning of a new relationship with people, with myself, and with God, as I began to learn just how much I needed people to love me and that it was okay to need people and their love.

*   *   *

The radio in the car jolted me back to reality. It had quit raining, the sky was clear, and I was closer to Corpus . . . to Portland. The radio once again reported that Corpus was totally sealed off; Harbor Bridge was closed to all traffic. I felt very disappointed now and couldn't put anything together as to how to get to Carolyn. No phone. No electricity. I knew absolutely nothing about where she was, how she was. And nothing about the sixty-five kids that I had been responsible for at the summer place in Port Aransas. I racked my brain to think of some strategy to use . . .

12

Color
Frogs
Green

Trying to make it to Carolyn reminded me how making quick decisions had been very much a part of my life. One day I had received a phone call from Bill Cody, a man who became a director of Laity Lodge. He called to talk about a little project that the HEB foundation had decided to put together. They wanted to know if I would be willing to help with these plans to coordinate a camping program. Bill and I met in Dallas in a motel and spent one whole day together. I had the strangest feeling about it when I climbed on the plane to fly back to Oklahoma City. I felt as though I had just met another kookie idea coming up the pike. Yet the more I turned it over in my mind, the more I thought about the kind of kids that could be involved there; and the more I was drawn to the idea that Christians had to get active in new kinds of projects.

Where I was in my own life made me want such a camp project to be extremely personal. I wanted it to be small; I wanted it to be Christ centered, personally centered, so that kids would have the freedom to make choices as to what to do and be. I wanted no pressures put on kids in attempts to have them make decisions. Ideas and concepts of love would be shared, and young people would be permitted freedom to fit each into their lives at their own pace. I received permission from Young Life to spend a month working to help with the program the first summer.

The next four summers were exciting times. The first year we only had fifteen or twenty youngsters in each session, but I was to see perspectives that I had been learning over the years take form in our staff, and I began to see that these approaches worked positively. No matter how hurt a person is, and no matter how bad a person is, or what kind of trouble he is in, no matter how wealthy a background or home he comes from, he responds to love and he listens when you share what Jesus Christ has meant to you in a very quiet and warm way. This was what we began to do in those camps. The very first summer, we saw kids come in that were not interested in the gospel, not interested particularly in God — who he was or what he had done for them — but we began to see these kids change. We saw them accept love, and we saw them give love, even those who had probably never loved anyone in their lives. The project became a burning passion in my life due to its potential and its possibilities. In the next four years, with the help of Bill Cody, Dave Philpot, and Howard Butt, and the great crowd of kids who attended as counselors and staff, we built those sessions into one of the most successful camping enterprises in this country.

Eventually every session of the summer was filled to capacity, and the number of kids returning year after year was phenomenal. We developed a new attitude toward camping in those who returned. I guess the most important experiment was being permissive with kids, letting them do what they wanted most to do, letting them choose the skills they wanted exercised and cultivated, the ones *they* wanted to develop. Having a warm Christian counselor personally involved in the life of each kid continually was important; that was something I had learned in Young Life. But now we wanted to take it one step farther: we wanted to see if we could tear down some more barriers and bring kids into making decisions on their own so that when they were confronted with Jesus Christ, they would be able to make their decisions about him and his love. I must say something here: I've never been interested in social work as such. I believe that anybody who goes anyplace and does anything significant in the lives of people must have a message, regardless of what that message is. Since I became a Christian, my message has been that the real answer to the meaning of life is Jesus Christ. That doesn't mean that everything is going to go well or be great. In some instances, as in my own life, I believe it is and can be almost the opposite. My life as a Christian has been a continual struggle to be what God wants me to be, to go where he wants me to go, and to do what he wants me to do.

In the fall of 1968, Young Life asked me to move to Corpus Christi, Texas. Don Taylor, our regional director, discussed with me the possibility of this move. Carolyn and I talked so often in those days about never leaving Oklahoma City because we loved it so much. We had lots of friends, things had gone along well, and we were deeply involved in the lives of so many people. We really had no desire to leave Oklahoma. I remember thinking so hard and so long that I reluctantly put the decision to God, telling him that I would go and I'd be the person he wanted me to be. Negative feelings plagued me — don't do it; you don't have to accept this reassignment. Carolyn and I debated all spring about what we ought to do. In some ways I think it was what happened to her in the hospital, the conflicts in her own life, that convinced us to leave Oklahoma City. Our kids were at a good age for a transfer: Cathy was going into seventh grade, and Scott, into fourth. It would be sad though leaving all the warm people we knew and loved. In a moment of anguish, I told God I wished he would just leave me alone. I wanted him to forget the whole thing — Oklahoma included.

But somehow in his great love, he reached down and loosened me up. I was able to make the decision: we would move to Corpus, without bitterness. The next two and a half years were the most lonesome years in my life. The hurt that had taken place in my life up until then, the hurt God had allowed to take place, was to insure my readiness for the pain that was now coming. At the same time, these were years of tremendous growth, years of expanding my thinking and extending my abilities. New relationships were formed, and feelings were found and shared in the expansion of my ministry which began in Corpus Christi, because now I was beginning to be able to receive love as well as to give it. Young Life, through some friends like Howard Butt and George Hawn, had been given a beautiful property on the beach at Port Aransas. They had begun to develop it as a setting for kids, knowing that Young Life had not done this kind of work in the past and knowing that little was going on anyplace else to help kids on the beach. So it was my responsibility to move in and research the possibility of a right way to go.

The move to Corpus was a good one. It gave Carolyn an outlet in finding a new home and decorating it. A beautiful new home, something she had always wanted, was a dream come true, for she had never had this opportunity before. For me it was a traumatic experience, to say the least; I had to make a new bunch of friends. My old fears began to plague me, especially in my relationship to kids, which had been so good in Oklahoma. The prospective relationships seemed at a distance and tough to instigate. The loneliest place in the world if you're not known is the halls of a large high school. I didn't want to go to a new high school and start a new Young Life club. I didn't want to see any new faces; I didn't want to get it going. It was traumatic to think of putting myself on the line again where there was a chance I could be a failure. Once again I was vulnerable — even to the point to being "destroyable." Because God and Carolyn had broken through my shell of phoniness, I was soon ready, but I was really vulnerable this time. Somehow in his great love, God gave me the strength and the courage to begin anew.

One of the things that made the move so significant was discovering how much kids had changed in the last few years. I woke up in Corpus to a whole new breed of teenagers; the kind of kids I grew up with were no longer around. High-school scenes had changed completely; I had to go back and do my homework — to find out what today's kids were like. How could I get to know them, become part of their lives, be able to minister to them the gospel of

Christ? Out of this came a new sensitivity, an awareness of the kind of world that we were now living in — a world alive in a different way than the one I grew up in. More facts, more things to do, more places to go. A whole new generation had grown up around my feet. Somehow I had to fit part of it into my life.

Young Life had been in Corpus for about six months before we arrived and was off to a good start, thanks to the capability of Rusty Palmer. Although I was excited about the opportunity of beginning a new Young Life club — my baby — I wasn't too excited about doing this at the age of forty-one. Going into a high school I'd never visited, not knowing a single kid in those halls, was scary business. But I knew I had to go, develop those contacts, and initiate relationships, so that we could begin the kind of friendship muster Young Life believes is needed — person-to-person. At least the haunting fear of failure was dimmer; I thought I had reached the point where I was free to be myself and not worry about failure to such a degree that it detracted from my ability. But when I finally involved myself with Ray High School in Corpus Christi, I discovered that I had *not* reached this point at all; I was *not* free to fail after all. I had made some steps in the right direction, grant you, but that old ego combined with that repetitious word *success* still demanded Frog Sullivan to do it better than anyone else. So I began my new ministry with mixed feelings.

I will never forget driving into that back parking lot at Ray High School, seeing all those wild, long-haired kids. I recall walking down the hall to the cafeteria and having kids stare at me and snicker. The old clichés were dropped: "Hey, look, there's the new queer" or "There's some old man over there trying to pick up some of our girls!" or "Look! We've got a new pusher in school!" If you want to find out what the word *loneliness* means, just go to a high school and walk around it for a few minutes without knowing a soul. You may be part of a crowd with all those kids stirring around, but if you don't know them, you can be *alone* — stranded! But things began to happen in that school before long. I was going to the football games, places where the kids hung out, and gradually began to talk with many of the youngsters. A lot of people had become excited about Laity Lodge and Christianity, and I found a group of parents eager to work with their kids but in need of some leadership themselves. So on the sidelines I was getting support from these parents.

We moved to South Texas toward the end of August, and by the first week of December, after almost three months of working to know kids, I began the Ray Young Life club. The first meeting was at Paul Shirley's house, and I'll never forget how scared I was. I knew that no one was going to show. I didn't want to go, only to find no kids, because then everyone would find out the fellow they had relied on as a leader was just a failure himself. But I managed to arrive a few minutes early to deal with my fears. Paul was a young Christian kid who loved his friends and had a lot of faith. When I arrived, I saw he had moved all the furniture from the living room, expecting a big crowd. I found it hard to believe since I had been so pessimistic about the evening's turnout. His excitement was contagious, and I began to feel more optimistic. That night a lot of kids came — sixty-nine— and we had great fun. Many I had never seen before, but I was anxious to get to know them. We sang songs, and they listened to me for a few minutes, and a new relationship with some extremely talented kids began. Three very important friendships developed from that group. Howard Butt, III, Paul Shirley, and Jackie Etheridge all became close friends of mine. Jackie was to have a particularly profound influence on my life, as a lot of kids have had. You know it's not numbers that make successes but what we do with "successes" and "failure." That night I gave my life as I felt God wanted me to. I'm convinced that he wants us to give ourselves to each other and make the world a better place in which to live.

I learned a new lesson that night: trying and giving yourself completely to an idea and giving yourself to Jesus Christ is important. These young people seemed to like hearing about Jesus Christ and his love in an intelligent way, in order to help them understand his care and concern. They liked hearing this from a caring, concerned, loving adult who had no axe to grind and who was willing to accept them where they were. They seemed to like the idea that I was willing to build relationships, with their care and concern uppermost in importance during that building process.

It was a fun year, and the kids responded; they became a major part of my life. My relationship with Howard Butt, Jr., nurtured with mutual respect, began to flourish because of my relationship with his son and the Laity Lodge youth camps. I believe that as a result of the Ray Young Life club, I grew much in the success-failure syndrome. If people were willing to accept me, great! If they chose not to, that was okay with me, at least it was not devastating. There were some other things which materialized from this Ray association. I recognized the many changes in kids of that generation. There was a new generation and a generation gap of some proportion — the "Now Generation," with hard rock, long hair, and beads. But they were lonely.

The sin of our age is that we don't believe what we say. We don't live by the professings of our voice. I had always talked a lot about being free, but I hadn't lived as a free person. I often spoke about God coming to give me real life — not just an eternal one. I didn't really under-stand eternity since it was too far out for me. But God so loved the world that he gave his only begotten Son that whosoever believes in him shall not perish but have everlasting life. And I saw that this means, not only eternal life, but real life, right now! I saw a brand new level of eternal life, a new way of living that begins the moment you open the door to Christ. Fac-ing these open, searching kids made real life begin and become a possibility for me.

I identified with lonely kids because I was lonely. The Corpus Christi kids and their com-munity made it difficult for me to develop new friends. Now I can look back and see my distaste for developing new relationships because of my desire to remain in Oklahoma City, where I was secure.

On my trips to Austin, I shared this with my friend Keith Miller. It seemed difficult for me to develop real, gut-level, depth relationships with my peer group. But a great thing happened. There was a Thursday morning group of men who had been meeting for a long time, and through Dr. John Etheridge and Charlie Brown, I was invited to have breakfast with them. We shared our lives with each other for an hour, closing with prayer. One of the most meaningful and helpful times for me in my whole Christian experience was this Thursday morning group over a period of four years. Leveling with fifteen guys, struggling with life every Thursday morning, sharing their theories, their failures, their successes ... crying, laughing, reaching out, trying to love and understand one another and where each was in his relation to God, family, the world ... these men ministered to me in a very special way. Their sharing reawakened my desire to know others and acknowledge my need for them. Those breakfasts were a place to get mad, a place to cuss, a place to pray, a place to say "I

blew it!" Most of all it was a place where we
affirmed each other, where we gave each other
a hard time, with the experience of that small
group bearing witness to our own mortality. It
was a healthy experience of knowing that God
cared and that other men cared about me and
their community, their friends, their churches.
They were busy struggling, trying to commit,
and attempting to give their lives to God every
day: they wished to be his people.

Just to know there are people like that in a
community is great strength to anyone trying to
work with people. These men had results in our
community through their influences, and I
found myself wishing for more groups like this
to allow many more people to open up and
share the hurts and frustrations of life with
others in need. At this time and in this group,
John Etheridge and I became good friends. He
is a man of maturity in many ways, with depth
and calmness — a definite opposite of me. He
and I began to share love together, and he
began a ministry to me in a very real way. He
will be a very special person to me for all time.

13
Frog Heads Home

As I headed toward Portland, I thought of how good the move had been for our family. For the first time, traveling had been a minimum; I spent much more time at home during the evenings. I had been involved with family projects and enjoyed the home we had purchased just a block from the Corpus Christi Bay in a quiet community, Portland. There was something good about all this.

Carolyn and I had always been very close, and as a result of having the privacy of a home

some distance from my work, my relationship
with Carolyn was the best since our marriage.
Finally, I let Carolyn love me, and I loved her
in return. We shared and tried to be honest in
our feelings for each other. We had in no way
reached the heights in our marriage, and we
still had wild "knock-down-drag-out" fights, as
people can have, because both of us were
volatile people. We got angry; we blamed each
other for mistakes. Naturally, in those moments
of frustration and anger, we reached out and
hurt each other, *and* we hurt our children. But
even in this explosive atmosphere, our relationship grew. I could now truthfully say that
once again we loved each other.

I was trying to be real, trying to let both
Carolyn and the kids know that I was no
"superperson," that I needed them. This was a
very difficult task. To admit weakness had
never come easy for me, and this was a continual confession of dependency. But my
strength came as I recalled how much God had
loved me and that he had died for me as a
human being — not only as God or a perfect
Christ — and that the glory of God was being
fully alive, loved, and cared for by him as just a
particular person, not as a plaster saint. So I
could now be worthy in his sight. Man, those

were the kind of feelings I liked in my life and in my home atmosphere.

In our new home, Carolyn, Cathy, and Scott needed me and I needed them. The beautiful thing that takes place in love meant everything in my life. My life became more authentic. Most people who loved me loved me for the things I had done for them. A lot of this was my fault: I made people *need* me! I believed that people would love you if you could create for them the fact that they needed you. If you had a talent or something special they needed, or believed they needed, you could attract them. I began to realize that love was not perfect. Love comes out of insecurities as well. Karl Olsson has meant a tremendous amount to me in this area, for he says that it's all right to love out of our insecurities. It's okay for me to love you if I need you. And it was okay for me to love Carolyn and the children because I needed them, which I did. It's also perfectly all right for me to love the world since I need the world — as a "Christian" as well as a "person."

I felt my entire relationship with Carolyn, Cathy, and Scott had been overhauled. We loved each other much more than ever before. I know that's easy to put on paper, and how I wish I could say here that now "we've done it" and now it's over with — but, of course, it isn't! This is a day-by-day, one-day-at-a-time, confrontation between individuals who share together, work together, and are not so desperately afraid to fail together — to find out all about each other for fear of not being accepted. Man, this was a difficult thing for me to learn and practice.

Somewhere in my background I had formalized the idea that one can never be satisfied with himself unless there is constant pushing and moving onward — doing, going, ever onward and upward. Achieving! Achieving in the society around us! Had I ever been an achiever! The performance group — man, that was me, all the way! Perform here, perform there, perform any place people expected. It had been ingrained into my very fiber that you worked; you didn't sit around enjoying yourself when there was a big world out there needing your presence. A Christian had no time to be idle. A Christian had to be doing something for somebody all the time. I was just full of my "responsibility" as a performing Christian. And like many Christians, I felt that *what* I did and *where* I did it were the most important and satisfying parts of life.

I had a behavioral neurosis that insisted

upon performance, constant performance. Not having experienced much peace in my life, just moments here and there taken at random in the middle of my activism, it seemed unnatural to question my usual appetite for perpetual motion. How could I get rid of this feeling that made me so uneasy and left me feeling guilty when I had any leisure time on my hands? I prayed about it, trying to give it over to God — with little success. But still it churned and burned on my insides. That insistent feeling and nagging that told me to get busy and do something productive, to be on with it, to move forward, improve your situation, master each day better than the one before. You have to perform to a higher degree. You've got to be better than the pack. These rules were rooted deep inside me. They had either been taught or I had learned them through previous experiences. I suppose I learned many of these attitudes in athletics. There is a strong contention in most sports that you've got to be better today than you were yesterday. You must score faster and higher than the other team or individual and dig in just to stay on top; perform and be the big winner! But now I'm not sure at all that that's true for everyone.

At last in our home in Portland, I began to

become a little freer, less hung-up on performance. I was learning to be comfortable at night with my family. I didn't feel guilty that there was no place I had to be and no one I ought to be talking with about something or other. The guilt-feeling that I ought always to be doing something with regard to my work was less intense. I acknowledged to myself that it wasn't wrong to enjoy my family. That was a beautiful conversion for me!

*　　*　　*

The radio was blaring at me, convincing me there was little chance I could get to Portland via Corpus. Harbor Bridge reportedly had been closed, and, approaching Mathis, I began to have this terrible sinking feeling as I spotted effects of Celia. Branches of trees had fallen, blocking the highway and bounding me around as I drove over them. My mind, weary from tension, began to play strange tricks with reality. I was aware there were no lights any place along the roadside. The hurricane had demolished Mathis just before I got there. I pushed the panic button, frantically searching for a plan of action. There was no place to stay in Mathis and no sign of anything much to do. I remembered a back road from Mathis through the little communities of Odem, Taft, and then Portland. Would there be any chance of slipping through the roadblock by that route and getting into Portland? As I sped down that little road, accelerator to the floorboard, the voice on the radio offered some encouragement: even though Celia had been a horrible hurricane, there appeared to be few fatalities. I heaved a sigh of relief upon hearing this piece of good news out of the mismash of facts gathered by the media. Surveying the devastation, I wondered why I had moved to Corpus Christi in south Texas in the first place. It had been a hard decision to leave Oklahoma City. Scott had been playing baseball, and it had been great fun to watch as he enjoyed his games. I even coached a few of them and found I enjoyed being with him, sharing his pleasures and disappointments. Cathy had involved herself with a neat group of girls while playing on the elementary softball team. Some of those contests were just too comical for words. I almost laughed aloud as the image took shape in my mind. I found myself enjoying the children, being with them, becoming a real part of their everyday lives.

During those moments of despair, worrying

about what had happened to Carolyn during the hurricane, the relief of recalling some humorous incidents in my life seemed inappropriate, but necessary. I turned to the many happy moments that had flashed through the void, tugging urgently at my life strings. God was beginning to calm me some, and I began to pray for some decision as to what next to do. In the middle of my prayer, I looked up to find the roadblock immediately ahead. Without hesitation I blasted straight through that hurdle, pulled a hard right, and skirted down the road through the middle of Mathis. I sped through the edges, with the highway patrol or sheriff hot in pursuit, siren and red light flashing with hypnotic menace. But there was no way he could catch me. There was not a car in South Texas as fast as this one, and I maneuvered it with directness of purpose.

As I hit a log and knocked it out of the way, I glanced through the rear vision mirror to see my pursuer come upon that same log. He hit it, and it slowed him down right away, as I moved on rapidly. Suddenly, I was jolted as my car leaped over a second telephone pole lying across the road. As I glanced once again into the rear-view mirror, I was relieved to find there were no red lights following anymore.

I had only been on this road once before so it was difficult to remember the way. There were no lights anywhere. It had taken me only about five minutes to lose the police. Why I wasn't killed that night I'll never know. I slid along the length of a third pole, my front wheels slamming to the pavement and the pole slipping along in front trying to slide out of the path of my madness. For some reason God evidently wanted me to make it this trip and did I need his help! I began to get frightened, for I knew there was a possibility that I was lost in the darkness of unfamiliar territory. Finally I came upon a sign, "Odem's Cafe" and a flood of relief came over me. I was on the right road.

But then it happened! There smack in the middle of the road ahead stood the sheriff with his flashing red light twirling atop his cruiser — waiting for me. I knew I was caught; there was no way I could escape. Running a roadblock, resisting arrest, speeding away from an officer of the law — these were all punishable crimes. I would probably get five years in a penal institute for this one. I had basically been a dramatic performer along through the years, and in my determination to accomplish things with positive results I learned to perfect my "con" ability. I recall praying to God at that moment, pleading for him to get me out of just one more scrape, for I didn't honestly think I could con my way out of this mess on my own.

I stopped the car with a feeling of defeat; but, nevertheless, I jumped out and ran to my captor before he had a chance to say anything. I didn't tell him about the roadblock, but only that I had driven from the hill country trying to reach my wife who was alone in Portland. I implored him for understanding of how desperate I was to get there, for she needed me now more than ever before. I shared with him my conviction that Carolyn had most likely been blown away along with all our earthly goods. Fortunately for me this man turned out to be a most understanding human being, and as he saw the frantic state I was in, he asked if he could help in any way. After looking at my driver's license, he said: "Mr. Sullivan, now you just calm down. You're okay! I'll tell you what I'm going to do. I'm going to let you go on ahead, and I'll radio to the other roadblock at Taft and tell them you are coming. They'll let you through to Portland. Now Portland has been hit very badly, but there are no deaths reported; it's just blown all apart. I want you to be extremely careful, for there are trees across the road; power lines and telephone posts are down the entire distance from here to Portland."

Since I already knew this and had hit most of them by then, I only half-listened; my mind was rushing ahead to my next move. He continued to announce his intention of letting me pass if I would be very careful. Then he added a friendly gesture which took me quite aback: "I'd go with you but for the fact that some nut just ran the roadblock at Mathis a few minutes ago, and at the speed he's barreling along, he'll be here in about five minutes. I'm going to catch that rascal!" Upon hearing that, I quickly thanked him and leaped back into the car, heading for Portland once again at top speed. Of course that sheriff was looking for me; I was that rascal he wanted.

14
No Castle, Just Home

I drove on to my destination, handling the wheel simply by habit as my mind was preoccupied with the past and memories of Carolyn and the children. As I came upon some power lines down in the middle of my path, I noticed two fellows standing along side their car, gazing down the road. Automatically I slammed on my brakes and, in a state of irritation, pulled up beside them and asked what they were waiting on. They told me they were afraid to cross the power lines because they were full of electricity. "Well, I'll tell you what," I said. "I'll stand on them and hold them down while you drive your car across." I pointed to the other fellow, asking him to drive my car across as I continued to hold the lines.

Those guys' eyes widened as big as saucers; I think they must have thought I was sent by God. What they evidently didn't know was that when a power line falls, it has a breaker on it that interrupts the flow of electricity. So, to their amazement, I stood on the lines and they drove both our cars safely across. I then jumped back into my car and took off laughing as they still stood beside their car shaking their heads in disbelief. How long they had been standing there I didn't know.

I flew through Taft and accelerated into Portland, both rear tires squealing. As I drove into that little community, my heart sunk inside my chest. I couldn't believe the damage before me. It was a quiet evening; nobody stirred. The dead silence of tragedy surrounded me as I drove down streets where once-beautiful homes stood. House after house was blown apart or completely lifted off its foundation. Nothing but a few two-by-fours jutted out sadly on a lot where once a structure had been supported. I just couldn't take it all in, couldn't believe the picture my eyes beheld. Since it was a dark night, it was difficult to make out the turn onto our block, but as I peered up the street, I saw that three or four of our neighbors' houses were totally gone. My heart in my throat, I pulled into the driveway of our yard and through the darkness could hardly tell that there was anything wrong with our house. (Later I found that we had fifteen thousand dollars worth of damage.) I rushed out of the car and attempted to fling open the door. It was locked; so I began knocking wildly, in great anguish. From behind the door came a meek little voice asking, "Who is it?"

I yelled insanely. "It's me!"

And Carolyn replied: "What in the world are you doing here?"

I thundered through the door and grabbing her to me, hugged her in the renewed knowledge that she meant everything to me. I encircled her so tightly, feeling that little warm body of hers against my own, and as I did, I thanked God that we were okay. The house? We could build it back. Carolyn and I were together; we had each other, we had our children.

The next morning as we sat in front of our house which was partially blown apart with windows missing, all rugs and draperies ruined, ceilings that had vanished with the wind, Carolyn turned to me and said, "You know, things are not important. The important fact is that we have each other."

That morning I realized that the meaning of Christianity lies in our human authenticity; we must be able to express our feelings for one another and not be afraid to commit ourselves and our love for each other. Saying "I love you and I need you" to each other is vital; tomorrow we may not have the opportunity to share our feelings. Tomorrow we may be called to another level of life. Carolyn and I both expressed our belief that while things have their place, *people* are precious, priceless, valuable as recipients of God's great love. I knew I had to learn to treat them more nearly as that! As we stood out front, arms around each other, she looked up at me and with tears in her eyes said the neatest thing ever: "I'm so happy you're home!" I knew what she meant: she was glad I loved her enough to come home to her.

That's when I came home to my family — physically, mentally, and emotionally. Right then God made all that very real to me. I'd been so busy loving other people and building a "home" for others that I'd somehow failed to come home to my own family. I'd never wanted to stand guilty of passing by someone who wanted my love and not sharing that one commodity "I love you" with them when needed. It's not difficult to say "I love you" in this world in which we live. I wished to share God's love and our love with him. I felt that people are important. People are the ones that God died for in his agony. I saw that in reality it's only God that can eventually bring you home, as he did for me on that very contemplative morning.

Yes, God brought me home that day! That experience allowed me to begin to accept people where they are and to become much more tolerant in my everyday dealings. Love is such a warm, exciting thing. I hadn't been able to express my feelings to other people because of fear that someone would reject me. I know it's our feelings (good and bad) that we're all afraid to put on display. But we must learn to do it! At least, I must. I love you — those beautiful words roll off the tongue so easily. When I say them, I mean that to love is to commit myself without reservation. I am interested in your happiness in all things; I want to help you when you need it, just for you, as you are right now. I'll try to help you work out those needs; and if you need just to talk, I'll listen. If you need to listen, I'll talk. If you need the strength that comes through human touch, I will touch you. If you need to be held, I'll hold you.

Two or three weeks after this awakening, Carolyn and I recognized our closeness and how deeply aware we had become of touching each other. We liked it so much more, for it seemed to carry a message of understanding between us, a new way of communicating our love and caring for each other. I wrote a poem that helped me share what I felt when we say "I love you."

> I miss your touch, it's been so long,
> How long can long be?
> A day, a night, a month, a year,
> Or maybe just from touch to touch.
> Touch me quick — I love you.

If we're ever going to reach out in our world, I'm convinced we must love more personally. We must give love to receive love. This kind of love is making us more sensitive to life; it makes us aware; it hones our being to a keen sensitivity for others. As Keith Miller has said so many times: "It makes us so vulnerable!" But we've got to be that way; as I love people and touch them, somehow they're going to recognize that God touched my life and made it an expression of his love. I must seek . . . I must touch . . . I must love . . . I must give . . . I must receive — and not necessarily in that order. If I don't practice these beliefs as a Christian and as a person, I will die, and a part of the world will die with me. I want to become a true loving spirit, rich in the love of God. I want to transmit a spirit that loves other people along with God, loves life and loves the world in which it exists. I want to share with this world in which I coexist, God's message of love (God's life changed) — which became my own on a frantic journey through the storm of a lifetime.